# By Death Parted

# By Death Parted

*The Stories of Six Widows*

Edited, with an Introduction by

**Philip Jebb**

**ST. BEDE'S PUBLICATIONS**
Petersham, Massachusetts

LIBRARY OF CONGRESS CATALOGING IN PUBLICATION DATA

By death parted.

Contents: Introduction  /  by Philip Jebb — On win-
ter's hill  /  Joane Rittner — Emmanuel, God is with us/
Margaret Adams — [etc.]
1. Widows—Great Britain—Biography. 2. Bereavement
—Religious aspects—Catholic Church. 3. Widows—Great
Britain—Religious life.   I. Jebb, Philip.
HQ1058.5.G7B9   1986          306.8'8          86-10244
ISBN 0-932506-45-3

Our very grateful thanks to
Dom Philip Jebb, our editor,
for his constant help and guidance

# Contents

# Acknowledgments

The authors and publisher wish to express their gratitude to the following for permission to include copyrighted material in this book:

Dom Philip Jebb, unpublished poems.

Dom Philip Jebb, poems from *Widowed*, St. Bede's Publications, 1984.

"The Mystery" by Ralph Hodgson reprinted with permission of Macmillan Publishing Company from *Poems* by Ralph Hodgson. Copyright 1917 by Macmillan Publishing Company, renewed 1945 by Ralph Hodgson.

Sonnet no. IX of "The Heart's Journey" from *Collected Poems, 1908-1956* of Siegfried Sassoon published by Faber & Faber Ltd., 1958, p. 180. American edition © 1918 by E. P. Dutton, renewed 1946 by Siegfried Sassoon. Reprinted by permission of Viking Penquin.

Excerpt from *The Will and the Way* by L. P. Hartley, published by Hamish Hamilton Ltd.

# Foreword

The common experience of every widow must surely be a sense of aloneness. However much support is given by family and friends, nothing can touch this isolation in the early days of widowhood. There is no relief from the sheer weight of sorrow, the feeling of apartness from all natural happiness. The following pages do not bring words of comfort, but they bring the touch of companionship as a widow recognizes her own experience in these poignant stories.

Widowed in my early twenties, one of thousands who received the news by a War Office telegram, after forty years I can still identify with each account. Whether, like Mary Whyte, we have had years to prepare for the moment of death, or whether it has come as a sudden blow as it did to Joane Rittner, we have all had to cope not only with the agonizing sorrow of bereavement but also with the shock of adjusting to a totally different status and lifestyle. Having shared the initial experience with these six widows, I found that I also shared many of the stages which followed—the "extraordinary tiredness" described by Susan Wheeler, and the struggle to conform to the pattern of life around one. Mary Thorold describes Christmas as "the most lovely feast when the whole Christian world celebrates the birth of a baby—yet it is the loneliest, saddest time of the year," an annual effort. With Margaret Adams I suffered again the bitterness of having no children and the often painful steps toward religious conversion. There is the resentment, there are the temptations to despair, and so many of my thoughts and feelings are recalled vividly by Maire Tugendhat's collection of letters.

Two Scriptural figures helped me very much in the lonely period of rehabilitation. The first was Job whose long dissertations seemed appropriate and somehow comforting—the extremities of his blessings, losses and eventual rewards appealed to my sense of the ridiculous even while I said with him, "The Lord has given and the Lord has taken away—blessed be the name of the Lord."

After I became a Catholic and could begin to see my sufferings as part of the sufferings of the Cross, I prayed often to Simon of Cyrene who, according to legend, was rewarded for his services on the way to Calvary, albeit unwillingly given, by the gift of faith. Acceptance is a necessary step towards peace of mind which leads to contentment and the receptiveness to joy.

Ten years after my husband's death I was accepted as a member of a religious Institute and had the opportunity to make another total dedication of my life. If the blessings I received were not as spectacular as Job's, they were not less rich and included a new family and even many children—those who are in our care.

The Church, in her prayers for those in need, commends to the faithful "the helplessness of the handicapped, the anguish of the incurably sick, the failing strength of the aged, and the grief of widows." Through no choice of our own we have the painful privilege of being among those who have left the world of natural happiness, taking a special share in its sufferings, carrying the cross of Christ. Let no one imagine that grief fades, but it can be transformed so that it is borne willingly and even joyfully.

In the following pages each widow tells her story of growth in faith, renewal of hope and a rekindling of love.

Sister Mary Denis Radley, IBVM

# Introduction

There are over three million widows in Britain today. Each one in her different and highly personal and individual way has had to cope with the shock of losing her husband, and then with the business of continuing and reshaping her life.

This book records the experiences of six women who have lived through this agony. The circumstances of age, family, preparation for widowhood, and the resolving of their problems are very different, but they share in common their religious belief and their desire to help and encourage others who find themselves widowed. It should be of very real help and encouragement for women who have not been prepared for their loss, and perhaps even more it will provide a vivid and practical insight for all those who are called upon to be a help and support to widows, whether they be doctors, nurses, solicitors, social workers, samaritans, priests, or simply friends and neighbors. All of us, at sometime in our lives, are going to be called upon to be close to, and to help some wife who has lost the father of her children. But sometimes through a sense of inadequacy, fear of intruding, shared shock, or simple ignorance, that help and support is withheld, or not given in a constructive way.

This book does not begin to cover all the possible circumstances, and still less does it provide all the "answers," but through these very clear, very brave, and very genuine witnesses a pattern does emerge of what a widow must go through, or may go through, and what this particular handful have found a help or a hindrance both in the first days and, what in some ways is the harder time, much later.

We see the three classic and progressive stages of bereavement: numbed shock and intense grief, followed by the different attempts at building up a new life without a husband, and finally the leading as near "normal" a life as possible while remaining single but remembering a companioned past.

In these accounts we see so vividly recalled the moment of death and the immediate reactions, often so incongruous: the sense of unreality, the seemingly endless demands of the telephone, of officialdom, of the children. This is the time for silent and practical help, perhaps more naturally and easily provided by women: the casserole, the flowers, feeding and distracting the children, just physically holding on, or being in the house at night. But men also can help: answering the telephone, providing ready cash, dealing with the undertaker. . . .

The funeral is a critical moment for it makes the first stage in breaking with the past. The advice of Monsignor Bruce Kent to get it over quickly has much to commend it. After this will come in most cases the first attempts at consciously living alone, and that awful experience of nearly all widows of returning to an empty house alone. If there are dependent young children their demands will force the widow to action and reaction, but if there are none or if they have already grown up and have left home, there can be the struggle to assess and to face up to changed circumstances. There can be terrible feelings of being out of one's mind, of being (understandably) "only half there," guilt and remorse at the failures and mistakes of the past that cannot now be put right, resentment at being left alone, perhaps with little money and with great worries. Decisions are being forced upon her at a time when she is in no fit state to take them. Again the advice here offered not to rush into ill-considered decisions is wise. Widows should be listening to advice, but should do all they can not to surrender all their will, not to go against deeply felt instincts.

At this time there will be many tears, often uncontrollable, and the widow should not be ashamed of them, nor her friends distressed by them. They are an essential part of the grieving process and it is wrong to think, "If I give way now I will never recover." Again, the part of the good friend is to be *there*, close by, physically holding, seeing that something is eaten reasonably regularly. Perhaps making a regular pattern of visits or telephone calls or letters to which the widow can respond and begin to order her life. How right is the comment that it is not enough to be told by people "I think of you"; so much better to show it by visiting, by phoning, by inviting out. True friends are not going to be put off or surprised by sudden changes of mood, by rebuffs, by alternating weakness and strength.

Decisions will now have to be made of a momentous nature: selling some property, moving to a smaller house, getting a job, perhaps changing schools for the children. Widows will need help and advice coupled with patience, courage, and gentleness on the part of the advisers. And while these advisers must show sympathy and understanding, they must also remain clear and rational and not be overwhelmed by the emotional upset with which they are dealing.

This second period after the death of a husband can vary enormously in length and intensity as well as in its circumstances. There is the pain of anniversaries, of facing what to do with the dead husband's clothes and other personal belongings. An early element in this part of recovery is acknowledging letters: it may take several months, but it can be a real therapy to concentrate on those who knew her husband and how he now lives on in *their* memories and experiences as well as hers. Conversely, it is clearly of great importance to write to the bereaved, however inadequate one feels over how to do it.

The other suggestions and experiences are very significant and important at this stage: getting involved in some new or well-practiced occupation like gardening, clearing out the house, calligraphy, drawing, music, visiting others bereaved and suffering and consciously helping *them*. There is so much that the widow can do by way of sympathy and understanding and becoming a samaritan or a bereavement counselor. "Never withhold what can be given. A closed face instead of a smile can put the finishing touch to misery." For the Christian also there is prayer and the belief in the Communion of Saints and the conviction that the dead husband is still a real part of her life, supporting and even influencing by his unseen presence.

This second period imperceptibly merges into the third, when life as far as possible returns to "normal." All these six authors, by their very writing of their pieces and their ability to reflect upon their experiences, show that this can be achieved and how it has been effective in very different circumstances.

Now there is the need for their friends and families to concentrate on treating them as persons and individuals in their own right, not simply labeling them with the title of "widow"; ignoring previous evidence of imbalance and emotional instability; asking them out to parties, even though they refused earlier, or were inadequate when they came; making a conscious point of remembering how there is a deep-rooted social bias in favor of the single man at the expense of the widow; realizing that she needs positive support when she arrives alone at any gathering; understanding that anniversaries are still important, though they do not necessarily need explicit mention. Finally, letting them know that they can be called upon to help in a really significant way when others are suddenly widowed, for they have the ability to listen, to give practical advice from their own experience, and they are a living proof that life can be lived again.

This is an inspiring, fascinating, and most important book.

Dom Philip Jebb

# By Death Parted

The Lord does not ignore
the widow's supplication
as she pours out her story.

(Sirach 35:14)

# On Winter's Hill

*by Joane Rittner*

Stephen, my husband, had not been well and had spent several days in bed. It was a Monday morning when we discussed whether he should remain in bed for lunch, and having decided that he should, I went to fetch his tray. On my return I found him dead. The kiss of life, a priest, a doctor, were my immediate reactions, followed by the problem of finding my four children: Mark and Susan were in London, Simon in Hertfordshire, and Luke at school in Wales.

The breaking of this news was an agony, and the many telephone calls prolonged and difficult. The parish priest and doctor arrived while I continued with evermore complicated phone calls to relatives and immediate friends.

Looking back on that traumatic, eternal Monday I seemed to be floating like a dried sponge on turbulent waters. The phone rang incessantly, people came and went. One friend, I remember, brought me an enormous bunch of daffodils, another a casserole, another whiskey. It is a brave person who takes their courage in both hands and approaches so close to death. How grateful I was to them, and indeed still am.

The dread of meeting the children as they returned home one by one was overwhelming. I was incapable of talking, and so were they. Somehow we managed—all four were so brave and supportive.

Night's deep desert, goading the fearsome hours
Leers at lone heart, weak for bright day's powers.

(Dom Philip Jebb)

I was forty-nine, and that night, the first of many dark nights, I slowly realized through the sleepless hours that my life had already changed. The pain and suffering that lay ahead were better for being veiled by the tears of the moment.

Weeping may tarry for the night,
but joy comes with the morning.

(Psalm 30:5)

But it was many a night before joy came with the morning.

During the long months that followed I was acutely unhappy, both spiritually and mentally. I felt totally unbalanced, as though missing a limb. Wherever I was, or whatever I was doing, the loss of that ordinary everyday companionship of some thirty years, which was whipped away overnight, was a lasting and unbelievable experience. I was lost and alone.

This aloneness drove me temporarily (I hope!) to a semimadness. I remember doing such extraordinary things quite out of character. One of my favorite escapades was to visit as many of Stephen's relatives and friends who could bear with me—even to the length of calling on his family's retired gardener (who went by the excellent name of Winter), leaving him and his wife, I expect, in utter astonishment at my unheralded visit. On another occasion I visited his old home—a very foolish move. And once I crept to his grave searching for help and strength—while tears flowed, I remembered happier moments.

Weeping was a constant problem. Now I say to people (who so often are ashamed of their tears) that tears are simply the opposite of laughing, and must not be scorned, but used as Our Lord planned. How much better one is for a good cry—even though it may stem from self pity—it is better out than in.

> Did you my poor one weep on Winter's hill?
> Dreading the fearsome cold of landscape bare?
> Did you feel you'd had your fill,
> And wonder how the Lord could care?
>
> Does grey salt spray from ever lifting seas
> Hammer less harshly at the castle's sand?
> Will it not listen to our failing pleas
> As urgent waters eat the recumbent land?
>
> But restless Ocean lays the rocks anew
> Adding the marvel of a fossil's form;
> The sap will soon our darling woods renew
> And bring us glory in the tingling storm.
> Those tears that spring from keenly mourning eyes,
> Flow down for you to streams in Paradise.
>
> (Dom Philip Jebb)

My material problems were endless, often seeming insurmountable. The decision to sell my house was a relief, which was fortunate, as many widows who are forced to make such a change find it hard and painful. I could not bear the constant "feel" of Stephen in the house. Yet I wanted to be near and to feel him, but not in the way the house offered. Something deeper was needed, prompted by prayer and the acceptance of Stephen's sudden death. But my acceptance was nil, and my prayers intolerably sluggish, meaning little to me. The dry sponge continued to bob about on the ever choppy waters. I could barely mention Stephen's name or see his photograph (even as an infant) or be near his possessions, without weeping.

During this bleak rootless period my close friends stood by gallantly, always at hand. Mark, Susan, Simon, and Luke were wonderful. Two special friends gave me strength in the light of their own long widowhoods, and for the first time I was aware of their many years of courage.

> My soul went waterless
> Over the harsh rocks,
> Down the dry valley of poor heedless stones,
> A tunnel to my tomb.
> No tears to shed in that bleak world,
> But only a stumbling on through desolation's symbols.
>
> The first lift comes with the green fern,
> Springing to the hint of light.
> Then mist, and the rising of water,
> The boulders rounded by the calling stream.
> The falling path now leaps to the sun.
> Oh, the glory of the Day new found.
>
> (Dom Philip Jebb)

After a long, black, and deep despair a small chink of light broke its way through, giving me the experience of human sympathy and understanding of a rare depth. Through this heaven-sent gift I learned by slow degrees to relate to the Good Lord again and to pray without as much bitterness as I had experienced before. The dry sponge was softening, soaking up the knowledge that where there is love there is pain, that they go hand in hand, and that it is impossible to have love without pain. The true and only means of alleviating suffering (and I repeat alleviating) is to accept it in a positive way. This is far from easy, but the persistent pulling away, resisting acceptance, only makes one's sorrow harder to bear. I know to my cost.

This linking of love and pain applies in many smaller issues of everyday life. It is preparing us, perhaps, or giving us a taste of what the future may hold for us. After all, our marriage vows include "Till death do us part," but how many of us dwell on those words at the time of marriage, when we are deliriously happy, and living only in the present?

> Today with its unseen alloy
> Awaits the fire-trial of tomorrow;
> The vows Love makes in days of joy,
> Love keeps, with moan, in nights of sorrow.
> (Fr. Vincent McNabb, OP)

Through the spiritual guidance I was receiving I now seemed able to pray just a little and the dark despair was slowly vanishing. Spiritual balance (if there is such a thing) seemed nearer, bringing with it a peace that I had not experienced for several years, but I was still not only alone, but lonely—two very different things. The visits of my children were inevitably less frequent, and the long weeks became emptier.

On the advice of a wise friend I started to draw, and how grateful I was, and still am, for such advice. Not only was it all-absorbing, with the hours rushing by, but the whole countryside took on a new magical aspect; the hills, hedges and streams I saw through different eyes, and I had a great urge to get them on to paper. The quality of the sketches was unimportant. It is wonderful therapy which is to be recommended even to those who say "I can't draw a straight line." Who wants to draw a straight line?

But still there was time to spare, so for a year I worked two days a week in a small hospital. This also helped financially, which was very necessary at the time. Others' sufferings are often a temporary cure for one's own, and my heart bled for the old people who depended so much on the kindness and good will of those in authority. They did not always receive the kindness they deserved. My eyes were opened to a small new world; I was often surprised and incensed at the petty injustices which took place.

It was around this time that I was able to plan the conversion of my farm buildings, dating from about 1620, with the help of my youngest son, Luke. We designed two small houses, one of which I now live in. This was a great challenge, and very absorbing, releasing the few creative powers I possessed, and which had lain dormant for so long. It was fascinating and rewarding to watch what had once been cow stalls, milking parlor, and loft transformed into a well-proportioned elegant house with ample facilities for enlarging it should there be need at a later date.

It is a great advantage to have a pleasant outlook, and even better to have a good view from one's house. I am more than fortunate with my fabulous panorama which faces south over an exquisite valley and hillside patterned with deep twisting lanes, the shadows changing minute by minute. The plow of today and then tomorrow's crackling stubble all mesmerize me like the sea or flowing water. I just gaze transfixed, lost to the concerns of the moment, and sink into a great open chasm—all the while being brought closer to God, to Stephen, and all my beloved friends who have gone ahead of me to Paradise. I seem drawn into eternity, and find I am reluctant to return to face the day again. But when I "come to," I pray earnestly that all my friends are lining the heavenly corridors for my own (I hope) eventual reception!

Some time before the house conversion I was asked if I would start the Downside Abbey Bookshop and Gallery. This was a very formidable proposition, for with the exception of a few months in the Times Book Club during the War (most of which was spent *under* the counter avoiding the V-1's and V-2's), I had had no such experience.

However, the Book Shop gradually got under way, becoming mainly a religious shop which was badly needed in the middle of Somerset. It is great therapy and extremely interesting, not only from the angle of administration and buying, but also from the people I meet day to day; very often old friends come in (one came into the Book Shop not long ago and we had not met for fifty years!) together with many new acquaintances. Frequently I am advised by helpful monks over the choice of books, which is a great bonus, lessening my responsibility as far as reading matter is concerned. I have learned much of the art of dealing with customers, and the psychology of selling. The red-letter day is when a kind person praises the shop and appreciates the problem of buying the right things for a varied and unknown public.

Sometimes I feel the Book Shop is rather like a hairdressing establishment where customers under the influence of heat and subsequent relaxation often talk. This I regard as an honor, and sometimes just to listen from the other side of the counter seems to help. I also find myself an unofficial guide, directing visitors to various parts of the establishment: the Abbey Church, the Monastery, the Head Master, the Bursar, the Guest Wing, the Tailor, and so on. The absence of signposts and helpful signs are quite a feature of Downside, but a constant nightmare to visitors!

Of course there are times when black depressions tend to take over, but the "aloneness," so hard to bear in the early days of widowhood, is now almost an essential part of my life. I find often that too much of too many people can suffocate me, and I must free myself in order to breathe again.

Is this the moment to touch on the constant returning to an empty house? How many, I wonder, find this one of the hardest experiences of widowhood to be endured? Often have I flung open the front door and listened to the silence. But what a bonus when, as if by magic, I find a son or my daughter or a friend sitting patiently in the garden, waiting for my return—but this is exceptional and the empty house must be faced. Gradually it becomes alive by flinging open the windows linking it to the ever-welcoming garden, or by lighting a fire so that it spreads its glow and warmth to every corner of the room. This, together with my own movements, sets alive the once peopled home.

Pure silence drops from Heaven
only when the heart is still.
Alone, alone, my soul,
come to the unending centre:
be drenched
by the desert's single eye.

Look out across those mists
sheeting the peopled world at dawn.

Remember the fenlands:
dark lonely soil
with solitude complete
between the treeless dykes.

The quiet at home
with only the even ticking of the clock
and sparrows under the eaves,
noisily selfish to the last.

Here is deep calm
From the rippling pressures of the world.

Here drink,
and find the welling fount within

where you can meet
full surcease of violence
and God's enfolding arm.

Hear secrets
from before the everlasting hills.

Find strength
for all the business that must follow.
Your garden is enclosed.

(Dom Philip Jebb)

There are naturally worries, anxieties, and disappointments which have to be borne alone, but prayer and a fairly regular daily Mass give me that inner peace of mind which builds up the grace and strength necessary to accept the crosses that come to us all (not only widows) during the course of the lifetime.

A great sorrow at this time was the death of a beloved sister, and not long after, sorrow struck the family again when Susan's husband died after a sudden illness. I stood on the sideline of her suffering, and that of her two daughters, gasping at her monumental courage and endurance.

Finally, I moved into my converted cow stalls. Then I took to developing into a garden the large concrete farmyard, whose only vegetation when I arrived was a vast, succulent growth of nettles. It has been the therapy of therapies. I can strongly recommend gardening in any form—a window box if needs be. The touch of soil, stone, or even the despised weed: all have the gift of healing tension and anxiety. I become completely immersed. Again, while gardening (as when drawing) the hours fly by, and I am driven reluctantly into the house from sheer exhaustion. Gardening is also a wonderful means of communication. Many of my plants have been given to me by friends, some a number of years ago, forming a chain of continuity and bringing back a memory of the friend, the place, or time when the plant or cutting was given. And what a conversation piece a garden is—I am always learning something new, such as the excellence of sprinkled Epsom salts on any shrub or rose! What immense pleasure it gives; no matter how simple, how large, how small, it is a joy.

### The Mystery

He came and took me by the hand
Up to a red rose tree.
He kept His meaning to Himself
But gave a rose to me.

I did not pray Him to lay bare
The Mystery to me,
Enough the rose was Heaven to smell,
And His own face to see.

(Ralph Hodgson)

Of course, like hundreds of other widows, I often long for that silent companionship which is the essence of true understanding. Nor do I forget such memorable words as "Goodnight Darling"; the small compliment, "That color suits you," or "I'm taking you out this evening"; the surprise small present; and the indefinable look across a crowded room "Shall we go?" or "Come and rescue me."

The evening and weekends are the vulnerable times as so many of us know. They are also important to most families when for a day or two they all manage to be together. With this in mind I try not to encroach on a family circle unless I am specifically invited.

I think it is worth mentioning here the number of my widowed friends who so often tell me how difficult they find it to be constantly the extra woman. To any hostess such a person is an embarrassment. On the other hand, an extra man is a bonus and an asset to any party! Womens' lib or not there is simply no answer to this. The widow must eat the crumbs of the rich man's table, and stretch her sense of humor just a little further!

But a wonderful bonus which must on no account be forgotten is the ability to listen, learned through one's own experiences. One can often help others, particularly those recently widowed who perhaps are still floundering and groping for balance and advice.

Give me understanding that I may live.

(Psalm 119:144)

So my life has continued for twenty-two years. In 1961 I wondered how I could endure even one year. But I have learned how one is never asked for more than one is able to give, even though I found the effort at times almost unbearable, and I have felt stretched to my utmost limit.

I am forever grateful to those special close friends and my children who so nobly stood by me, who have constantly pushed me along to my new life and new horizons.

Is widowhood then a means of finding oneself? Or finding others? It is certainly a means of finding God.

O Lord, thou has searched me and known me!
Thou knowest when I sit down and when I rise up;
  thou discernest my thoughts from afar.
Thou searchest out my path and my lying down,
  and art acquainted with all my ways.
Even before a word is on my tongue,
  lo, O Lord, thou knowest it altogether.
Thou dost beset me behind and before,
  and layest thy hand upon me.
Such knowledge is too wonderful for me;
  it is high, I cannot attain it.

Whither shall I go from thy Spirit?
  Or whither shall I flee from thy presence?
If I ascend to heaven, thou art there!
  If I make my bed in Sheol, thou art there!
If I take the wings of the morning
  and dwell in the uttermost parts of the sea,
even there thy hand shall lead me,
  and thy right hand shall hold me.
If I say, "Let only darkness cover me,
  and the light about me be night,"
even the darkness is not dark to thee,
  the night is bright as the day;
  for darkness is as light with thee.

For thou didst form my inward parts,
  thou didst knit me together in my mother's womb.
I praise thee, for thou art fearful and wonderful.
  Wonderful are thy works!
Thou knowest me right well;
  my frame was not hidden from thee,
when I was being made in secret,
  intricately wrought in the depths of the earth.
Thy eyes beheld my unformed substance;
  in thy book were written, every one of them,
the days that were formed for me,
  when as yet there was none of them.
How precious to me are thy thoughts, O God!
  How vast is the sum of them!
If I would count them, they are more than the sand.
  When I awake, I am still with thee.

(Psalm 139:1-18)

# Emmanuel
# God is with Us

*by Margaret Adams*

When a dearly loved husband goes on ahead, you are faced with a crisis of the greatest magnitude and need extra help and strength, as well as consolation, so that you can pick up the threads and continue the journey through life. And continue you must, for you still have to work out your salvation.

A time of crisis is a time of hope; now you are offered another opportunity for renewal of your spiritual life and this will give you the strength you need. The renewal will probably be different for each of us. The following story tells how I became aware of the power of the Holy Spirit and how my spiritual life was renewed.

\*       \*       \*

When, at the age of sixty, I became a widow it seemed to me that there was nothing left to live for. I felt I was the only widow in the world; others there may be, but they had children and I had none. I really felt sorry for myself and thought no one could possibly understand my feelings or problems.

"I'm a widow," I said to myself. "Oh, how could he go and leave me alone? What am I going to do? How can I go on living? Ever after this, Christmas will be a sad time, for that is when Harry left me."

His last illness was caused by a stroke and he had three months of terrible suffering before he died. I cried so much and dreaded meeting people in case they asked after

Harry—I couldn't explain without breaking down. After his death I would go out to do the necessary shopping and on my return put the car into the garage and stay there weeping before plucking up courage to go back to the empty house. I did not tell anyone of my feelings. Perhaps it would have been better if I had, but I am a person who bottles it all up.

Through all this terrible time which comes to so many women, I had one very special blessing: the support and friendship of Stanbrook Abbey, a community of Benedictine Nuns, and a great powerhouse of prayer, which is their chief work. Later in my story you will hear how I came to meet them. They were praying for me in my widowhood and it was a great comfort to know this, and it made up for my feeble efforts.

The Abbess of Stanbrook gave me a book called *Widowed* by Dom Philip Jebb, Headmaster of Downside School. At first, being at the stage of not thinking clearly, I didn't feel he could possibly know what we widows suffered as he was not married. After reading this book several times and finding it consoling and helpful, I had to write and tell him how mistaken I had been at first.

> Jesus, you wept over the death of Lazarus,
> and felt abandoned in the face of your own,
> give therefore to us who must live with this
> searching spear deep in our hearts, the all-
> conquering power which draws all things to
> yourself, and which is your risen life. Amen.
> (Dom Philip Jebb, from *Widowed*)

This brought me nearer to God, and somehow, even though it seemed impossible to settle the problems which arise with widowhood, I thought that help would come.

There was also the feeling that although my husband was no longer with me, he cared about what was happening to me. I was not abandoned, although alone in the house and more or less waiting for the next thing to happen.

Many other people helped as well, especially Geraldine Squires who was on the staff of the Moseley School of Art where my husband had been Headmaster. She came down to visit me and gave practical help, and also telephoned once a week (and still continues to do so). It is a valuable help to know that a call will come. Once a term she has taken me to a hotel for a meal and at Christmas she has always had me stay with her, or she comes to me. What a faithful friend she has been! My next-door neighbors used to invite me to supper every Sunday after Evensong at the Anglican Church to which I then belonged. I also had two friends in Malvern who always gave me a friendly welcome to their house which has been like a second home to me. Another friend, who came for several days to help with nursing Harry in his final illness, makes an expensive train journey to spend a few days with me every year.

*       *       *

Before my marriage, I had been a student at the Birmingham College of Art and had studied lettering and design. The tutor was C. Harry Adams who was later to be my husband. He was a wonderful teacher and took endless pains with everyone. The training I received there was to prove very useful in the difficult years of widowhood.

I was able to continue my craft of calligraphy and design when I was married and later was elected to membership in the Society of Scribes and Illuminators. One day a letter arrived from our Secretary in London asking if I would like to go and see the Printer at Stanbrook Abbey near Worcester and give a few lessons in gilding letters on their special printed items. My husband and I made frequent visits to our weekend cottage in Worcestershire, only six miles from the Abbey, so it was easy to go along and meet Sister Hildelith who was in charge of the printing department and anxious to develop the "Fine Printing" for which this house has become very well known. What an interesting visit this was, although I felt very nervous!

Afterwards, Sister Hildelith wrote to thank me for going and asked if I would gild some letters for them on a small prayer they had printed. I was delighted to be asked. The prayer was:

> Lord Jhesu Crist, that madest me
>> That boughtest me on rode tree,
>> And fore-ordainedst that I be,
> Thou knowest what Thou wouldst do with me;
>> Do with me now as pleseth Thee,
>> Amen, Jhesu, for Thy pyte.
>
> (The Eton Prayer by Henry VI)

Much of my work involves religious texts and it is easy to understand how one's mind begins to think about the written words.

I had long been pondering my Anglican Faith and feeling there must be more in Faith than I knew of. We used to have religious discussions at home in my childhood, but being the eighth of nine children, I was only allowed to listen! Some members of the family were "High" and some "Low Church" and it confused me more and more. I can remember asking my eldest sister who went to an Anglo Catholic school, "What am I, if anyone asks?" When I grew up this question still puzzled me. I never felt comfortable about it and was always searching. So being invited to Stanbrook Abbey and having "The Eton Prayer" to work on, started my search in another direction. "Do with me now as pleseth Thee" was food for thought.

I had never known any Catholics before and it opened up a new world to meet people whose lives were centered on the search for God through work, prayer, and contemplation. Work connected with the Printing House was fascinating, and was not I helping in a small way with my gilding and design? Prayer meant little except formal prayers in church on Sundays. Contemplation was a closed book to me.

During one of our discussions, Sister Hildelith said that I needed to educate my mind and lent me a book called, *Treatise on the Love of God*, by Saint Francis de Sales, which simply amazed me, never having read anything like that before. When it came to returning it to the Abbey, I didn't want to let it go and was told I could keep it. Bede's *Ecclesiastical History of the English People*, Julian of Norwich's *Revelations of Divine Love*, *The Cloud of Unknowing*, and many other books also helped me.

Our home was in Edgbaston, near the Oratory where Cardinal Newman lived and worked. Hearing so much about the shock of his "going over to Rome" from my Anglo-Catholic sister, it now occurred to me that I ought to read his *Apologia* as part of my education. The Birmingham Public Library produced an old and mustysmelling copy. This book convinced me utterly and there have never been any doubts in my mind since then. I knew which church I wanted to belong to in order to continue my search for God.

"Do with me now as pleseth Thee." Ah! There was the challenge. Could I rise to it? Perhaps my mistake was in thinking it all had to be done by me. I still knew little about the power of the Holy Spirit and prayer.

Lord, be the beginning and end
of all that we do and say.
Prompt our actions with your grace,
and complete them with your
all-powerful help.

(Prayer from The Divine Office)

The difficulty here was my husband's avowed dislike of
Catholicism and his anger and dismay that I should want to
do something which would divide us if I became a Catholic.
We had a very happy life together and it filled me with
misery to think of hurting him. I am sure that in all honesty
he thought he was saving me from making a great mistake.
He enlisted the aid of his great friend to drive home his
point. With two such forceful characters ranged against
me, the situation became impossible. I gave way and realized my weakness, which is a humbling experience.

It was suggested by my dear friends at Stanbrook that it
would be best to put the whole thing out of my mind for
the present. Things would come right in the end if I
remained faithful and kept hope in my heart, and they
would continue to pray. What a comfort this wise advice
was; but all the same, it was impossible to forget.

I was still asked to do work for Stanbrook and the loving
kindness and encouragement given by the Abbess and
Sister Hildelith was far more than I could ever deserve and
I am eternally grateful for all they have done for me.

Interesting commissions arrived. Siegfried Sassoon was
received into the Catholic Church, and to mark the occasion Sister Hildelith printed five hundred copies of a collection of his poems; a gold initial was needed for the opening
page and a very special copy was prepared for the poet
himself. Many other jobs were offered to me. What a
pleasure it was to drive over to the Abbey and deliver

finished work. On one occasion Harry and his friend were with me and said they would wait in the car. The Sisters told me to go out and invite them in for coffee and, much to my surprise, they accepted and thoroughly enjoyed talking to the nuns.

The time came for my husband's retirement and we bought a house at Colwall, near Malvern, on the Herefordshire side of the hills. After ten happy years in the house he loved so much, Harry died. We had been married twenty-eight years.

I felt utterly lost and sad, but various things had to be done and it was necessary to pull myself together and make arrangements for the funeral. This is a harrowing experience but somehow, something happens and you get through it with dignity. Two of my sisters spent a few weeks with me after the funeral, and went back to London, advising me to sell my house and look for something less expensive to run as I had been left with very little money. To be forced to sell the home where we had been so happy seemed the end of everything. I was feeling ill and very sad—not at all able to go through all the business of selling a house and finding somewhere else to live.

Being over-persuaded, and not knowing what else to do, I contacted a house agent who said he would sell the house when the daffodils were in bloom.

A few weeks later, feeling very miserable and lonely, I was tidying up things in the garden in case people came to view the property, when, just as I was trying to light a bonfire, a sudden message came: "Don't sell." Whether this was from the Spirit, my husband, or wishful thinking, I simply don't know, but it made me come straight back to the house and write a letter to the agents cancelling the sale. I posted it immediately and felt a lot better.

Dear Widows, I beg of you to do nothing in a hurry if you can help it. You have suffered a great blow and cannot think clearly. Pray without ceasing, for it will bring you nearer to God and he will help you. Also, the nearer you are to him, the nearer you will be to your husband.

Listen carefully to all the advice you will be given by well-meaning people. But say very little: remember that the final decision must be yours.

Getting in touch with Sister Hildelith to give her the latest news, she said, "Don't worry, what you want is plenty of not-too-difficult work." She sent along hundreds of hymnals to be covered. It was wonderful, as well as financially helpful, to have this work to do every day in addition to the routine household jobs. The books had to be delivered to the Abbey, which kept me in touch. I designed some cards of religious texts and had them printed. Orders came from Tewkesbury Abbey, Hereford Cathedral, Malvern Priory, and other places as far away as Canada and the USA. The words on one card were as follows:

May the Lord bless you and keep you,
May the Lord let his face shine on you
and be gracious to you.
May the Lord uncover his face to you
and bring you peace.

(Numbers 6:24-26)

The card was bought by a Jewish doctor who got in touch with me and later invited me to the Feast of the Passover in his home. This was a wonderful experience.

Through Stanbrook Abbey I got to know Joane Rittner who had seen my work and ordered some cards for the Downside Bookshop. We met for the first time when she was in Worcestershire and had time to call and see me. This has been such a valuable friendship. Other work arrived as people learned that I needed it and, gradually, with the help and encouragement of many kind friends, I worked my way into a more stable position. But rapidly rising prices were a worry and money was needed for house repairs. I was not earning enough to settle these problems and wondered if I could sell something in the house. Two small books I had inherited made me one thousand pounds, which I spent on having the kitchen modernized. Sister Hildelith, when told the news said, "Can't you find something else?" I produced an old book out of the attic which, with her help (knowing all the right people) made me eleven thousand pounds at Sotheby's. This book consisted of engravings on rice paper, by Matteo Ripa who was a secular priest attached to the Jesuit mission to the Chinese court from 1711-1723. They were views of the Imperial Palace and gardens in Jehol, Manchuria, and only eight known copies were recorded until mine turned up. The goodness of God has astounded me.

> Dear God, your generosity has been from
> without beginning and can have no end;
> so in that generosity we pray you
> to give us the vision and the power
> to make of all we have and are
> one great gift, that you may be our
> All in all, and that we may grow
> to the immensity of that gift.
>
> (Dom Philip Jebb, *Widowed*)

The Catholic Church still drew me like a magnet, but the thought of disloyalty to my dead husband worried me very much. Eventually I was told that we could pray for the dead and help them on their way by our loving support and that, conversely, we who are left behind and are still working out our salvation, can be helped and supported and encouraged by those who have gone before us. When I realized that Harry, now knowing the Truth, would be concerned for my salvation, there seemed to be no obstacle which couldn't be overcome.

When the right time came (God's time, not mine) I was better equipped to respond to the event which has been so great a consolation in my widowhood. Sister Hildelith instructed me and arranged my reception into the Catholic Church at Stanbrook on the Feast of the Assumption. This has filled me with intense joy which has never left me.

\*     \*     \*

From my experience I would like to give a few thoughts:

People will long to help you with sympathy, but often feel embarrassed about death and don't know what to say. Be gentle and try to help *them*. If they tell you about their troubles, listen carefully and don't say that yours are far worse. When you have recovered a little, make as many new friends as possible—never lose an opportunity, even if you don't feel like it, for it may lead to helping others. When you are sad and lonely it is quite wonderful how much better you feel if you go out with a smiling face and put aside your own troubles for awhile. This doesn't mean that you don't miss your husband—of course you do—but you have to keep this secretly in your heart. If you feel too ill to go out, there is generally the telephone, and a quick call to someone can make them feel not forgotten. I have mentioned before how much a phone call means to me. Above all things pray, then you will learn that however dreadful things are, God is with you.

> I will ask the Father,
> and he will give you another Helper,
> who will stay with you forever.

He is the Spirit,
who reveals the truth about God.
The world cannot receive him,
because it cannot see him or know him;
but you know him,
because he remains with you
and is in you.

(John 14:16-17)

# All Alone

*by Mary Thorold*

It wasn't death that was hard to cope with, it was life. My husband, Bernard, obviously knew he was going to die and I realize, with the benefit of hindsight, that he had prepared himself for it spiritually. He had always had a great affection for, and admiration of, Cardinal Newman, and in those last few weeks I often noticed him saying prayers for Newman's canonization, or reading part of his works. There was a general and increasing tranquility about him.

I, on the other hand, was not prepared. I do see now that I should have realized that my husband was not going to live into old age—but no one actually told me he was dying. Even on the very last day when I drove my husband to the hospital, he said, "Do you want them to tell you the truth?" to which I answered, "Yes, you know that I always find it easier to cope with the truth." As it happened, I was told that Bernard would be operated on that afternoon, and that I could visit him during normal visiting hours. I went home to clean up the house (we had just returned from a two week holiday in France) and to await the gas men who were to mend the hot water boiler. About one o'clock I went to do some shopping and to put some petrol in the car. When I got to the garage I was told that my petrol account had been closed by the company for whom Bernard worked. I was in a raging fury, and rushed to the hospital to spill all to Bernard. I couldn't remember which ward he was in—he had been in University College Hospital so many times and in so many different wards, that I tended to get confused—but I found him. He looked awful. His bed was cluttered up with tubes and machinery. I walked over to the window and looked out over the well-kept gardens of University College. It was such a beautiful, sunny September afternoon. Suddenly there was total silence. My husband was dead.

No one had told me he was going to die. If they had I should have fought my way through the tubes so that I could have held his hand to help him take those last few steps. I should have liked to have been able to talk to him: to say I was sorry for those times when I had been so hard on him (I *was* hard on him, as I believed that as long as he kept going all would be well, and so I forced him on and on and perhaps sometimes he would rather have been left alone), to thank him for the love he had given me, for the child he had given me, and—for my sake as much as his—I should have liked to have been able to call my parish priest. But I didn't know, and so very quietly at about 2:40 P.M. on September 3, 1979, Bernard died and I was a widow at the age of thirty-four.

Instantly my mind touched on three things: body, soul, son. I got a doctor for my husband's body, a priest for his soul, and I went to pick up my son, Crispin (aged six years and six days) from school.

My car was outside the hospital and despite protests from the nurses and doctors, I drove to the school to get Crispin. As I arrived I saw my parish priest, Bruce Kent, standing on his doorstep. The first miracle. He was always so busy that to find him at home was an incredible stroke of good luck. I told him the news, and said that I would bring Crispin in after I had broken the news to him. I also saw Crispin's headmistress, and agreed with her that Crispin should continue to go to school. She said they would be able to look after him and keep him occupied.

Somewhere in my subconscious I had obviously prepared myself for the moment of telling Crispin because it happened as I had imagined it would. As we walked the fifty yards to the church, Crispin kept asking, "How's Daddy? Where's Daddy?" Just before we reached the top of the steps I turned to him and said, "Daddy's dead." Hardly a second passed before Crispin screamed and screamed. We went into the church and I held him in my arms as he cried and cried. As the tears subsided we went and put up the first of many candles "for Daddy" and cried our way through a prayer.

Those candles were to be a very important link in our lives. I can remember a very much older woman once saying to me something along the lines of "You don't go in for that pagan nonsense do you?" Those candles were a lifeline—when we lit one it was a direct link with husband and father—and our little prayer was going up to him at a time when we were incapable of doing anything else. Although it doesn't happen very often now, we still don't feel ashamed about lighting a candle. It really is our hotline to heaven.

We then went in to see Bruce who was magnificent. When the funeral was over I remember writing to Bruce to say that he had been the silver lining in my cloud. He was totally sympathetic without being sentimental; he was practical without being in the slightest bit officious; and the love and concern he showed for us both is something that I shall never forget and for which I shall be eternally grateful. After producing a welcome cup of tea (and two hankies) he sat Crispin on his knee and asked what hymns he would like at Daddy's funeral. Crispin immediately chose the Lourdes' hymn (we only had three verses!).

Bruce suggested to me that I should hold the funeral as quickly as possible and he put the wheels in motion straightaway.

To anyone else in this position, I do think this is one of the most important bits of advice. There is no way you can begin to accept the fact of death, or begin to build any life, until the awful trauma of the funeral is over. Therefore, the sooner you get it over the better because life must and does go on.

My husband wished to be buried so we had a Requiem Mass and then a private burial. It was a lovely day—the sun shone, the flowers were beautiful, but the moment of burial is agonizing. And it lasts. A good fifteen months later, on one Sunday morning just before Christmas, Crispin and I were going to put some flowers on Bernard's grave. In the middle of Mass Crispin turned to me and said, "Do you think the worms have eaten Daddy's body yet?" I had no answer to that question, but silently vowed that I should like to be annihilated so there would be no funeral, or failing that, cremated.

The first few days of widowhood were unbelievable: the telephone never stopped ringing. Of course I had to make endless phone calls—my brother-in-law was in London as was my sister-in-law, although I didn't call her as I thought she was in Italy. Otherwise everyone was out of London. My mother-in-law was in Devon, my father in Kent, my Aunt in Holland, my brother in Canada. While I made these calls, my next-door neighbor took Crispin for a walk and gave him some supper. As soon as I had finished my calls, the telephone rang and rang and rang. The news was getting around and everyone wanted to talk about it. And then people began to drop in to see me—the whole week was really like one long cocktail party. I honestly didn't really know what was going on, but I did manage to organize the funeral.

I found that my memory went completely. I literally walked around with a notepad in my hand. Any suggestion or plan had to be written down. I am better now but find that I have never gone back to where I was before Bernard died.

Other memories of those first few days are concern about money. This situation was eased temporarily by my mother-in-law who came to see me immediately upon her return from Devon with £100 cash for me. She too had been widowed and could well remember the horror of actually needing cash and not being able to get it.

And then there were the letters which came pouring in. I think I received about 120 in all and, although at the time each one made me howl more than the last, I am very glad to have received them and am so grateful to those people who wrote. The reason for this is that I now have a marvelous picture of my husband encapsulated in those letters. Different people had appreciated different aspects of Bernard's character and personality and as one reads the letters through, the whole person comes out. (I have to admit that I have only read them twice: once on receiving them, and then about two years ago. I won't read them again until Crispin asks to see them as I am sure he will one day.)

Bernard was an enormous man with an enormous personality. He was very kind and helpful to people in need; he was always full of zest for life, and had enthusiasm for everything he did. This came through the letters so vividly. I always think it a shame when people say "No letters" for two reasons: one, as I have already said, although they can cause more sorrow, they can also be a great help; and two, because I feel that the "onlooker" must be given the opportunity to make some kind of comment, and we the sufferers must allow them to do that. One must learn to accept as well as to give. And of course, when one receives letters from friends, at least one knows that they have heard the news. The most shattering experience is six, eight, or ten weeks after the event to run into someone somewhere who says, "Ah, how's Bernard?" It is traumatic to tell them—and devastating for them to receive the news in this way because they are immediately covered with embarrassment.

I always try to write to friends of mine who have lost a relation. I never say much, but feel that having lost so many people close to me—my mother when I was twenty-four, my husband when I was thirty-four, and my father when I was thirty-seven—I do know what they are going through. I cannot say anything at all that will help, but just knowing that their friends have stopped for a moment in time to think of them is a great help.

There is then the dilemma of answering these letters. As people had taken the trouble to write to me, I felt they deserved a personal reply. (I can remember when my mother died, part of the therapy I devised for my father—who was in an appalling state of shock—was to write at least three letters a day.) I cannot remember what my replies were like—perhaps some days I was more effusive and friendly than on others—but I did reply to them and it took me a long time. I finally finished them in Holland at the end of October. I had gone to spend the mid-term holiday with my aunt, and she dispatched me upstairs after breakfast every day to deal with the correspondence before I could enjoy long walks along the beach. I came home at the beginning of November with a clean slate and, having achieved something, I felt much better for it.

Bernard died on a Monday, the funeral was on Friday, and by Friday evening everyone had gone and I embarked on a self-imposed weekend alone, at home, with my son. Sooner or later one has to come home to an empty house, to be alone, and so I decided to jump the first hurdle immediately. I still think I was brave to do this! But I also know for me it was the right thing. By nine o'clock on Saturday morning I was reading the newspaper—I couldn't think what else to do. I realized then that the days would be very long. Surprisingly I slept quite well once the funeral was over—I was very tired after six long years of first a baby, and then a sick husband. Possibly I was relieved that so much suffering had come to an end.

Crispin has barely been mentioned so far but his presence was of the utmost importance. He was finally coaxed to sleep, on that first day, at about midnight by Bruce Kent. I went to bed soon afterwards—and realized with horror that I hadn't fed Crispin. I had taken great trouble to feed myself, but had forgotten Crispin. (I discovered the next day that my neighbor had fed him.) I vowed then that the most important thing was Crispin—he had be looked after and loved. The next morning I got up and deliberately dressed myself in decent clothes—oh, jeans would have been so much easier, but I was determined to keep some kind of standard.

Crispin was magnificent throughout. I could never, or would never, lie to him, and having told him straight out that his father was dead (what is the point of saying he has gone on a long journey?), he accepted the fact that he would never see Daddy again. He doesn't like it even now—he periodically has a bout of miseries—and in some ways I am pleased; at least his father really meant something to him. Equally, I am realistic enough to know that some of the miseries are because he is the odd one out, not having a father like other children, and at his age, no child likes that. To me he has always been, and is, a great companion and friend, and particularly so in those early days. He showed remarkable sensitivity and understanding. Often he would come up to me, put his arms around my neck and say, "I love you." One day I asked him why he did it, and he said, "Because you haven't got Daddy to say it to you anymore." He shares my griefs, my frustrations and— I hope—my joys. I know that I have made mistakes in all this because he has not experienced a trouble-free childhood. I don't think he'll ever look back on it as an idyllic time of happiness, but I am afraid I needed him, and he gave me what I needed. He has grown up a lot now and we don't have quite the same need of each other, but there is no doubt that he is much more aware of my life than his peers are of their parents' lives. I honestly don't think I could have made it without the impetus of my child—all my hopes and expectations are in him. But then I sometimes feel that I have absolutely nothing else.

During the first few weeks of widowhood, people were very good to me. We were visited, asked out to lunch and generally made to feel wanted. But a sadness or loss is personal, and other people's lives go on—they forget your emptiness and loneliness—and as the days turn into weeks, the weeks turn into months, the awful feeling of aloneness intensifies.

It was over a year before I faced the real crisis. I was busy in year one. First of all I had to find a job. We had never had much money, we were generally in a crisis situation, and so when Bernard died I had to do something about getting a job. At least that way I felt I was making some positive contribution to my future. I was very lucky to be accepted as an assistant secretary in the school next-door to Crispin's. This meant I could take him to school and finish in time to pick him up and also share the holidays with him. That really was a touch of the gods on my side.

I had a long tussle getting my life insurance money but finally it came through. I didn't particularly want to stay in the flat in which we lived because it wasn't "me." Also, the cost was too great and I needed a change—a new start. Suddenly one Sunday morning in January I woke up and thought, "I can send Crispin to St. Benedict's School in Ealing, and I shall buy a house nearby." There and then I set off to search for Ealing (I barely knew where it was!). In a very short time I had found a pleasant, affordable house, made an offer, and was in it within eight weeks. Crispin was accepted for St. Benedict's, and I found a job at a college in Shepherds Bush as a typist—again with school hours so that I could be with Crispin whenever he was not at school.

All of this took a lot of my time, there was a lot of organizing to do, many decisions to be made, and I more or less did it alone. I must be honest and say that it was not because people wouldn't help me, but as much as anything I think I wanted to prove to myself that I was capable of doing all these things.

We settled happily into our house. Surprisingly enough I had no regrets at leaving my home with Bernard—once they moved the furniture out, it was no longer home. The house was mine, and I had a garden. Every evening that summer Crispin would be in bed just after seven, and I would retreat into the garden and work. I got enormous satisfaction and solace from the hours I spent out there during that summer and I did feel very close to God.

Having achieved all of this I decided that we would visit my brother who lived in Canada and see some friends in the USA. My brother had been in Canada for twelve years and no member of the family had ever visited him. I felt Crispin and I both deserved a "grand tour," something totally different. And so off we went on our great trip! It was all so different—there was the sticky heat in Toronto, Washington, and Virginia; there were the hot dogs; the very friendly and welcoming people. After five weeks and a dreadful flight home, we returned to our own home—and were so happy to see it again.

Crispin started his new school, and I started the new job in September. And then we were settled, with new people around us at home, at school, at work—people who knew nothing of my husband and Crispin's father. No one knew of the anguish we had been through for so many years. Now I was really on my own.

Most of my friends have young families, their husbands are struggling up the career ladder. They don't have the time or resources to cope with an "odd woman." So many people used to say to me, "I do think about you," but being thought about is not enough. I should so much have loved them to pop in, or to telephone, or to ask us to lunch. I was very conscious at that time of invading the lives of others. I always tried to ring people at a time when their husbands were not at home. I had come to appreciate how precious those evenings alone with one's husband actually were.

As I was so young I did not have widow friends of my age. During my first few months of widowhood, the husband of a great friend was dying, and we were of benefit to each other then. There were older people I knew who were widows but I don't think I could relate to them in any constructive way as the whole situation was different. I had been married for less than eight years which was a very small proportion of my life. Those other people I knew had been married for much longer—their husbands had more or less seen their children grow up—but I was going to have to do that alone. I did contemplate joining a widows' group, but when I spoke to the organizer she said I would be the youngest by about thirty years, and that it would probably depress me even more—anyhow, I am not very good at group therapy. I am basically a loner and have to work these things out for myself.

I shouldn't let the very early days pass by without mentioning two people who were a positive influence and who, for very different reasons, kept me going. The first was my father. I don't think he ever really recovered from the sudden death of my mother in 1969, and he certainly could not cope with the concept of death. He was never particularly well and within eight weeks of my husband's death, he was in a nursing home. I had to pull myself together to visit him, and although he came home eventually, he was back and forth to nursing homes for the next three and a half years. But he was a distraction and he needed me very much indeed. He provided my son and myself with an escape in the country. If I ever got really sad I could always use the excuse of having to go see my father, and run away from the situation. He was an intelligent, amusing man who was very fond of me. Together we could sit the night through and put the world to rights. After a long struggle on both our parts, he died in April, 1983—another sadness as I had lost the last person who really loved me.

My mother-in-law also played her part in helping us through those early days. She was always positive and practical—as in the case of the money which I have already mentioned. After my husband had been dead about three weeks, I decided I must clear out his clothes and things, and so I asked her to come and help me. I thought this would be good for us both and it was helpful to me to have someone to share the decisions with.

I have often thought that perhaps my husband's death was even harder for her than it was for me because he was her child. How awful for a mother to lose part of her being—a husband is but an addition to one's being. She must have had many sad moments which she has hidden from me, and perhaps her other children. I tried so hard to recognize her great loss—in every death more than one person is affected. When a husband dies, the wife is distraught but so are the children who have lost "Daddy." There will never be another real "Daddy." At a time of death we really should remember to love our neighbor because everyone needs help.

As time has gone on the social situation has become easier. First, my expectations and desires have changed. Second, I have met new people in my "own right" as it were. It has been an uphill struggle but through my son's school friends I have made some good friends and they accept me as I am and they like me because I am me, not because they feel sorry for me. At work I have made new friends—we go to the theater, we swim, play tennis, or just go to the pub for a drink. Because I am a rather efficient person I have found myself in the position of organizing the Christmas lunch and other social activities at work. These activities helped me to make contact with people and I then found that there were people who had interests in common with me, so going to work isn't always a burden.

Crispin is a very lively and active child and has lots of extra-curricular activities—sometimes I feel there are too many, especially when the Thorold taxi service is in constant demand! But all his interests have opened up a new world for me. He is in the Cub Scouts and I am now secretary of the Scout Group which involves me in a lot of work, and gives me the opportunity to go out and occasionally meet people. I have been away on camping trips—until last year I had never slept in a tent in my life! And it was not as bad as I had thought it might be.

Crispin sings in Ealing Abbey Choir and that particular activity has meant that I am now in the rather nice position of being able to go to church and actually see some faces I recognize and know. Unitl this happened eighteen months ago I used to go to a church of strangers and that made me feel very lonesome, particularly as we had been in such a friendly parish before.

At school there are the parents' evenings—not really much fun as that is when you learn all your child's faults. But while waiting for an interminable time to meet the form master, you do meet the parents of your child's friends. This in turn means that when you go to pick up your child from school, there are recognizable faces and possibly someone with a smile and something to say. And then there are the rugby teas...and so it goes on and on. Of course all this will end one day, but in the meantime I have met people, made new friends, and hopefully they will remain friends for as long as we are neighbors. So given time, a little patience, and a lot of courage, things can be turned around, and life can take on a new dimension.

There are still moments which can be grim—anniversaries, birthdays, etc. I do think the impact of the anniversaries fades a little. Nowadays I feel a little down, but I don't have the awful sick feeling of past years. Perhaps it is good for us to have these dark times. It is important to reflect, to remember, to be thankful—and it is at anniversary times when the mind is totally focused on the missing person that one does these things. I don't make much of my husband's anniversary of death. My mother-in-law always remembers and sends me flowers. I am grateful for that although her kindness always intensifies my grief.

There are other moments that are hard to deal with. I always cry when my son is successful—partly pride, partly because I wish Bernard was here to see the success, and partly because I feel I have achieved something by the inspiration I have given him.

Then there is Christmas—the most lovely feast when the whole Christian world celebrates the birth of a baby— yet it is the loneliest, saddest time of the year. Every year (I have now had five Christmases alone) I have to make an enormous effort. I find Christmas shopping hard. I seem to wander in the crowds of happy families all making deci- sions together, with the *husband* carrying the bags! I can never decide what to buy and end up by almost resenting the whole thing. It is a time for being together as a family, for sharing old memories and experiences. I used to love our Christmas at home and I still try to make an effort with the tree and the crib, but the awful thing is that it is an effort. I would far rather take to my bed for a week and ignore the world totally. There is nothing like the complete silence and stillness of Christmas Day. It was once a time of wonder, now it is almost a horror—has the bomb fallen, are we the last two people on earth?

At the end of it all there is God. What role has he played? I frequently wonder why he "did this to me." Why should I be the one to struggle; why *my* husband; why this loneli- ness? I haven't, I'm afraid to say, yet forgiven either God or my husband for what they have done to me, and yet I know that I have the broad shoulders to cope with it and . . . yes, I find myself saying "Thank you."

Thank you for Crispin, for the joy he brings, for the

successes he has had, for the opportunities that my widowhood has given him, and for the fact that we both have had the courage to make the most of all the opportunities. There are many things which both of us have done which could not have been done had Bernard been alive. Crispin would never have gone to St. Benedict's, therefore he would not have gotten into the Ealing Abbey Choir. There is a chance that his musical ability would never have been discovered.

Thank you for the home and garden we have got—how lucky we are to have a comfortable roof over our heads. Thank you for my beloved aunt—she has stepped in as "Honorary Grandmother" to Crispin and as a totally unselfish, loyal friend and guide to me.

On and on it goes; there would have been different advantages and discoveries but not these. Somewhere in it all there is God. I can't say I am a very good Catholic—I sometimes doubt whether I am a good Christian—but I do believe in that Being who is responsible for it all. Without him there would be no hope, but I have yet to find the true peace that comes from a complete acceptance and understanding of God. I believe that as long as I can hold onto that fine thread there is some kind of hope.

The impact of death can never be understood until it has been experienced. You never "get over it," you simply learn to live with the new situation. You have to make a decision: shall I go on and live life to the full, or shall I cave in and be miserable? I have learned that while today may be bad, tomorrow could be better, and I try never to forget that "laugh, and the world laughs with you; weep, and you weep alone."

# A Horizon—
# The Limit of our Sight

*by Mary Whyte*

I have absolutely no doubt whatsoever that the best and most important thing which has ever happened to me was my baptism into the Catholic Church sixty-seven years ago in Newport (now in Gwent) where my mother was awaiting the end of the first World War and the return of my father from France. Although I know that some people regard my life as a tragic one, I believe that the flowing of that baptismal water and the wonderful gift of faith, which came through it later on, have helped me thus far to remain virtually unbowed under the heavy blows which have been rained on me. That was my first great stroke of luck, or, I should say, the first firm proof of the Lord's love and care for me, the beginning of his plan.

Twenty-three years later, during another World War, I had a second stroke of luck: I went to a small party given by virtual strangers and met there a tall, dark, handsome young officer in the Cameronians. His name was Alexander (Sandy) Raeside Whyte. We fell in love. As he said later, it was an immediate and all-embracing attraction.

In those uncertain and yet exciting days, it was difficult to look into the future—after all it might never materialize. We did not consider as deeply as we might have in times of peace; we were inclined to surrender to the dictates of the heart and the moment. The depth of our mutual attraction was nonetheless real, but it was based on immediacy rather than discovery, and we had only the most superficial knowledge of each other when we married on a foggy March day at St. James', Spanish Place, London.

God's plan for me was now really in motion. One cannot arrive at the state of widowhood without having first become a wife, and in order to reveal my feelings about being a widow, I think I must first try to explore the years of my marriage. It lasted for twenty-three years and from the outset was far from ordinary. I did not know it on that March morning, but I had married into a family suffering from the hereditary disease of the central nervous system called Huntington's Chorea (so called after the man who discovered it). In 1942, when we married, no one in either family knew this.

My father-in-law, an eastern merchant, had retired from Rangoon where he spent most of his working life, to a sporting estate in Scotland, where he lived until his death in 1946. The family doctor, a close friend, did not finally diagnose the illness until it was revealed in its most deadly aspect—only in the very last stages of life, when the involuntary movements increased so that he could scarcely be contained in bed. I am not sure whether all other family members—mother and two daughters—were made fully aware of the implications at the time, but I certainly was not, and it was many years before the horror of our situation was properly understood.

Sandy had gone to Sandhurst and was commissioned in 1939 shortly before the outbreak of war. He loved being a soldier and was proud of his regimental traditions, but he drank too much and got into too many scrapes and financial difficulties, and, as it turned out, he was forced to resign his commission. Not then knowing anything about Huntington's Chorea, which might have alerted us to the causes of his behavior, I'm afraid we blamed him—it was an awful time for us all. But he joined the Navy and by the time the War ended we had a daughter, Susan, aged three, and our first son, Nicholas, was born in 1946. Eventually we settled in Essex, and with my father's help Sandy was launched into study for a career in estate management and surveying, and was a pupil in a Colchester firm. Our second son, Simon, was born in 1948. All was going to be well—but was it?

We were happy with each other and with our family, and made many good friends, but several things marred our lives. Often Sandy returned to his old army habits of drink and irresponsibilty. He was sometimes restless, nervy, lazy, violently bad-tempered, unreliable, and useless with money. He was also not progressing as well as he should have with his studies and work. Finally, rather miraculously it now seems, he did manage to qualify, and in 1954 we moved off on a job-hunting safari for a couple of years, finally coming to rest with a partnership in a Gloucestershire firm. Our second daughter and last child, Prudence, was then four. We sent her to the village school, our eldest daughter was at my old Convent of Notre Dame, Teignmouth, and the two boys were very happy at a Dominican Prep School in Gwent. We settled into village life in our old cottage and hoped we were putting down roots at last.

Time passed. On the surface all appeared happy, but the disease was getting a proper hold, and we were enveloped in the resulting chaos—complaints and problems at work, and a very unhappy bank manager.

It was in 1955, shortly before our move to Gloucestershire, that at the suggestion of one of my sisters-in-law, we visited a specialist in London, who had diagnosed Sandy as being a suspect Huntington's Chorea sufferer, but no

details or implications were revealed, and the seriousness
of Sandy's condition was not realized. It was not until we
had a second opinion about 1957 that a crisis was reached.
The disease was confirmed: Sandy would never work
again. Our united families rescued us from immediate
material ills—my parents in particular being wonderfully
supportive—and we entered a new and frighteningly
uncertain stage of our lives.

I think that here it may be appropriate to try and give
some sort of exposé of Huntington's Chorea, because it
has a tremendous bearing on my whole story. It is
hereditary—passed on by a defective gene from parent to
child, with any offspring having a fifty-fifty chance of
inheritance. Its cause is unknown. Alongside and sometimes preceding the physical manifestations of loss of
motor control, changes in gait, loss of concentration, and
involuntary jerky movements, there may be marked personality changes. A lively person may become lethargic; a
placid person aggressive. There may be a tendency to dis-
orientation, wandering, or disregard for others' feelings or
even safety. After the disease strikes (possible at any time,
but usually in mid-life), it develops into the "slow, relent-
less, and irreversible physical and mental destruction of a
human being." Communication becomes difficult as speech
becomes uncontrollable and writing impossible. Intake of
food and drink becomes increasingly difficult, and control
of bodily functions may be lost. The involuntary movements can increase to alarming proportions, so that stillness can only be induced by drugs, which in the end kill.
Not all patients exhibit all symptoms, but it is almost in-
evitable that the sufferer will eventually require total
nursing care.

It may seem paradoxical that as Sandy's illness progressed, and the realization of its horror increased, so did our mutual happiness, and even towards the end, when only the eyes could speak, our mutual love was steadfast, and with the disappearance of our physical unity, our spiritual unity increased.

Though Sandy was not a Catholic when we married, we had never had religious differences. I had taught the children their catechism when we were living in the wilds of Essex, and we acquired a reputation for "praying to the Aga*," since we were often discovered by amazed and amused friends saying our family rosary and night prayers together in front of it!

I now realize that it was this constant praying together which not only kept my faith strong during many dark days and years, but also ensured that Sandy became a Catholic before he actually reached his deathbed. He was received into the Church in Winchcombe on All Saints' Day 1958, and he had the joy of participating with his children fully in the Mass and sacraments until he could no longer go to church. He was confirmed with our son Simon, shortly after being received, and while he remained with us at home, the family rosary and prayer session was moved from the Aga to his bedside.

I now knew that I would become a widow, but I had no idea how much time remained for us to be together. The next seven years were years of great happiness in the midst of great suffering. I knew that Huntington's and not Sandy, was to blame for past difficulties, and he had discovered spiritual peace and joy.

This period was dominated by a series of attempts to

*An Aga is a type of large stove which throws off a great deal of heat. (Ed.)

alleviate Sandy's sufferings—in the small ways we could each day, and in the wider field of undergoing treatments and operations which might prolong his life and/or serve as tests and experiments which might help other patients. Sandy readily agreed to whatever was suggested by the doctors, because he thought that through him something might be discovered to help future victims, among whom might well be his own children. So he became a virtual guinea pig in hospitals in Bristol and London—if anything helpful was discovered, it certainly did not help Sandy.

His sufferings must have been immense; brain surgery must be one of the least comfortable of operations. He never complained, and never faltered—he even joked about his shaven head and incongruous woolly cap, worn from time to time to hide the ravages. He himself spent a long time in prayer each day. We prayed together always, and his last six months in the hands of the Sisters of St. Joseph at Boar's Hill, Oxford, were agonizing but well-lived. The sisters loved him and were wonderfully devoted.

We last met together as a family on Christmas Day 1964, when we left him sleepily happy. Death came on February 25, 1965, beautifully, peacefully—a quiet slipping into the hands of God, who had come so mercifully to claim him. We grieved, but were glad, for as Bede Jarrett so well expresses it: "Life is eternal and love is immortal, and death is only a horizon, and a horizon is nothing save the limit of our sight," and at last Sandy would know the reward God has prepared for those who love him.

And then I arrived at the state of widowhood, which I had been contemplating for the last several years. The reality, the day to day prospect of that fact had to be accepted at last, and slowly, so slowly adjusted to, because I no longer had to care for my beloved. I was really the luckiest of widows because the Lord had given me four splendid reasons for working and living: Susan, Nicholas, Simon, and Prudence—my precious children, on loan from him to be my joy and hope.

We had a saying in those days, "We have done so much, for so long, with so little, that now we can do anything with nothing." The source of this quotation is unknown to me, but we thought it a pretty good motto. The mistake we initially made was in thinking we had "nothing" when in fact we had so very much: our faith, each other, and the knowledge and belief that the Holy Spirit was closely associated with us in all we did. In many ways those first years of widowhood were the happiest I had known—a strong bond of religion and love strengthened us and brought us many graces.

We survived materially as well. Throughout Sandy's last years, I was supported by the generosity of his family and my parents, and also by the financial help of the Benevolent Fund of Sandy's professional body, The Royal Institute of Chartered Surveyors. Susan was doing well in the Women's Royal Naval Service (WRNS); Nicholas was maintained at Stonyhurst by covenants set up by his godfather and my father; Simon was being educated through the generosity of the Carmelites in Cheltenham; and Prue's godmother, my old school friend Pat Burke, had come to the rescue so that she could stay on at her convent. The unfailing kind open-handedness of these heaven-sent relations and friends meant that we had a roof over our heads, and I was able to look for some gainful employment.

To begin with, I did easily acquired jobs like cleaning and cooking—jobs that I'd practiced for years at home. Then I went on to more exalted stuff like other peoples' dinner parties, and universal-aunting and nannying, away from home. I didn't really enjoy any of it, nor did it keep the wolf far enough from the door. Then out of the blue, Madge Lamplugh, a neighbor whose husband had been a house-master at Cheltenham College, came up with the news that the headmaster of the College needed a new secre-tary, and through her recommendation I managed to get the job. I had been trained as a secretary in London during 1938-39 and had worked at the War Office during the War, but since then had only done a bit of typing at home; so I was a trifle rusty. The headmaster was mercifully tolerant. I improved, and stayed twelve years.

As I have said, immediately after Sandy's death my fam-ily had many happy times together. We still went together to Mass when everyone was at home, and we often re-marked how great it was that we all seemed to revel in each other's company. I suspect we were all still benefitting from the shared experience of the sorrows and triumphs of Sandy's last days. Susie was obviously enjoying life in the WRNS. Nicholas had progressed from Stonyhurst to Caius College, Cambridge, and was studying medicine. Simon was at the Central School of Speech and Drama, doing stage management. Prudence as yet was still in her convent school.

Holidays were fun: we had a host of friends, old and young, who often filled our small cottage. We celebrated birthdays, anniversaries, feast days, Christmas. There were visits to Cambridge, and later to London when Nick got to Barts Hospital. He was keen on drama, and we were keen to be among the audience both at his productions and at the professional ones in which Simon became involved at the Oxford Playhouse, The Mermaid, the Old Vic. And we all wrote to each other a great deal—I still have most of the letters as a record of those amazingly happy days. It *was* rather amazing that we were so joyful with the sword of Huntington's hanging above us. I don't remember our discussing it much at all. The Lord was building me up wisely and lovingly for the next period of trial in his plan.

I can still most vividly recall Susie's tear-stained face when she came, alone, to tell me of her pregnancy. She had seemed the very last person from whom to have such a confession—the possibility of such a thing had never entered my head. So when she told me, I knew at once that Huntington's was with us once more, and that we all—but perhaps me especially—would again have to help a loved one face and journey through the same wilderness of suffering that Sandy had encountered.

Although one knows that whatever God permits for us must bring good if we accept it as part of his will, it is curious that it often takes us a long time to accept and cooperate in the challenges he sends us—they sometimes seem too much. But of course they aren't really, and when one has succeeded in accepting trustingly and humbly—and that's the difficult part—it is astonishing how things seem to begin slowly to work out.

Born in March 1943, Susie was a remarkably beautiful child, and grew into a lovely young woman. Though not academically brilliant, she was highly intelligent, and though rather timid by nature, she showed great courage and determination in overcoming her shyness. She worked hard at school and in the training she did later, and after some years in the hotel and catering world, she joined the WRNS where she did well and made many friends. She had a most loving, sympathetic disposition, and was always unselfish and generous. She had several offers of marriage, but never seemed able to take the final step, even with the father of her child.

I think her greatest suffering came from the thought that she had failed in some way to measure up to the family she loved so much. Now from her safety with God, she will know how wrong she was, and how it is we who find it difficult to measure up to the example she set us. She bore her twelve years of unbelievable trial with the greatest fortitude, and many people drew inspiration from her. Only last Christmas a dear young friend, studying for the priesthood in Rome, wrote to me that he had based his recent "preaching practice" on her—how she would have enjoyed that!

The joys and compensations of her stricken years really cannot be fully listed. There was the pleasure of being with her and her child Catherine, during the baby's infancy and early years, and seeing her joy and pride in her daughter. There were the countless acts of kindness and generosity from relations, friends, and even total strangers, who often approached her wheelchair, drawn perhaps by her youth and beauty.

She—we all—made many friends through her pilgrimages to Lourdes. We had been approached by someone hitherto unknown to us, who suggested we join the Ampleforth pilgrimage in 1974. This we did, and the annual visit became part of our lives, and is still part of mine.

Everyone just loved Susan—she seemed always gay and smiling. Her smile became famous, and still is. She surmounted the long periods of depression and what must often have been near despair, and was uncomplaining, patient, and resigned, drawing ever closer to God as she worsened in health. She was also close to her own dearly loved father, and together we often prayed to him.

Soon after Catherine was born we moved from our cottage into a house near Cheltenham College, which meant that I could continue to work and be close at hand all day long. Catherine went to nursery school at three, and for a year or so Susie managed, with the help of a sort of push-chair, to get to and from a small job she was given in the office of a local charity. This job came out of the blue through a mere acquaintance, and it was a lifesaver to Susie for awhile. But the disease progressed relentlessly, and the day came when she could no longer be properly cared for at home.

As luck would have it, a small chronic sick unit for young people opened in Gloucester under the auspices of the neurologist who cared for Susie, and there she spent four years, coming to us at weekends, until that too, sadly, became impossible. Perhaps her greatest sadness was her enforced separation from us all, especially from Catherine, but we always came away from our visits to her amazed at her cheerful acceptance.

She was particularly devoted to Father Leo Porter, one of the Gloucester priests, a constant visitor and support who anointed her frequently. The end, when it came, was mercifully swift, and her requiem was a joyous one. She is still so much missed, but surely she and her father are now with the Lord. The words of Edith Sitwell say it all: "Love is not changed by death, and nothing is lost, and all in the end is harvest."

Each survivor in a Huntington's family who has helped to care for, wept over, and surrendered loved ones, knows that although one sorrow is past, they cannot really relax. They mourn for each departed sad sufferer and then watch for, and expect, the next gentle reminder that the trial is not yet over, that God is still testing and challenging.

Some years before Susie's death, I recognized the dread signs in our loved and admired Nicholas. We had all followed his career with great pride, and he had slipped so easily and apparently willingly into his role as head of the family. We all rejoiced when he finally qualified as a doctor, and it was with almost unbearable sorrow that we noticed him changing. Formerly our mainstay and mentor, he now began to distance himself—his splendid faith the first casualty—and for some years before his marriage to Marion, all of us feared for his health and his future.

Between 1970 and 1979 family relations between Nicholas, Simon, and the rest of us were at their most strained. Nick married and seemed to want to sever family ties almost completely, while Simon married and divorced within four years, set off for Australia, and seldom wrote.

I prayed unceasingly that when the moment of truth came for Nick—as come it must—he would not reject God's challenge, and I admit that my own faith was so abysmally weak that I did not think he would be able to accept his fate. How ashamed I now am that I did not trust God enough in those days. I had forgotten all the tremendous graces Nick had received through prayer and the sacraments during the years of his believing youth, and that this great store of grace was now his to draw on. And he has, he has. He *has* accepted it.

I know the immense disappointment it must have been for him to renounce his calling as a doctor to become a patient suffering from a dreaded disease, with all the miserable humiliations it brings. I hope he is beginning to realize the rewards it may also bring. He is patient, incredibly brave, still the loveable, charming clown of his prep school days, visibly close to God, and from his privileged position here in the flesh, he is helping us all. I know this, and often during each day I try to join him in the prayers he may not even know he is constantly saying for us all, and of course Sandy and Susie join us as well.

Sometimes I ask Bernadette and her "beautiful lady" to lure him back to Lourdes, where he worked with the sick when he was young, to help him with the strength he will need for the final stages of his earthly pilgrimage.

Now to the third of my reasons for pressing on my widowhood with a will: Simon. At first happy and successful in his chosen career in the theater, charming his way through life with hardly a care, he married in 1970, too young, and was divorced in 1974. He spent the next four years in Australia with the woman who had then captured his heart, but the affair did not endure. He has always been a chap of tremendous enthusiasms, which have led him into and out of several "marvelous ideas."

The Australian years were followed by a study of acupuncture and an acquaintance with the world of health foods. He has now embarked on a second marriage to Katya, a Czech girl whose family came here as refugees in 1968. He is a full-fledged "Sanyassin," having been initiated into the cult of the Bhagwan Shree Rajneesh two years ago, and received a new name, Avrata.

All these different embarkations may be an escape route from Simon's fear of inheriting the family problem. They may also bring him at last into the right port—this is my prayer for him. He too has within him the reserve of grace from the happier days of his youth which, in the fullness of time, he may wish to call upon. Meanwhile, the dead, the suffering, and other loving members among his family and friends know they can leave him safely in the hands of the Lord.

My fourth reason for living, Prudence, born in 1953, has an impulsive, caring, compassionate nature. She is emotional, easily moved to tears, but far from insecure. She spent her senior school years at Cheltenham Boys' College (where I was secretary) and eventually graduated at Durham in 1975, later doing teacher training. She is now married to John Willday, a Cornishman sixteen years her senior, who taught her at the college, where he was a master for eight years before leaving to become Head of Economics at Norwich School. They now live seven miles outside the city, and they must have faith because they bravely decided to trust God, and have two children, Rupert and Rachel.

They all live, of course, in the daily shadow of Huntington's Chorea, and Prudence has been greatly affected by her sister's death and by the rapid decline of her much loved brother. She is not, however, overwhelmed by these sorrows, and busies herself in country activities, in her care for her husband and children, and with her many friends and the rest of the family. I am heartened to know that we have a close relationship, and I like to feel she counts on me not only as her mother, but as a friend.

Together she and I try to share in caring for Nicholas as often as we can—because we love him, but also as a help for Marion. Pope John Paul II, on his visit to England, said, "We should be with those who suffer," and from my own proximity to the sick members of my family and to those on my pilgrimages to Lourdes, I know just how valuable being close to them can be—an immeasurable aid in acquiring calm acceptance, courage to go on, and a little wisdom on the way.

I said there were four reasons for living, but there is another: for sixteen years I have been *in loco parentis* to my granddaughter, Catherine, born of Susie. The joys and trials of her early childhood have become the joys and triumphs of the here and now. She has been fortunate in acquiring a first-class education through a little persistence with the authorities, and a great deal of application, hard work, and success on her part. New Hall School has done her proud, and has helped with the balance of fees (paid largely by the LEA, the Royal Institute of Chartered Surveyors, and the Charlton Kings Higgs and Coopers Trust), and she has received sympathetic and devoted care in this excellent school. I'm sure large rewards await all these generous friends at the hands of the Almighty.

Now in the Lower Sixth, Catherine seems set for a satisfying career, perhaps in Law, via Classics at Cambridge (if she's lucky). All fingers, including her Mama's I'm sure, are crossed for her! I hope that one day she will know how much I admire the determination and courage with which she has so far tackled her young life, and I pray that she may have a secure and happy future, free from the family shadow. Perhaps God will follow through the gift of this child, who has been such a blessing to us, with the gift of good health for a long span of years. Our united prayer is that before long the researchers will penetrate the secrets of our disease and find a cause and a cure, as they have done already in so many other fields. I'm sure God must have this in mind.

When I retired from the College in 1979, I was persuaded to take up local politics. I fought and won, and have since won again, in the Borough Elections, and emerged as an Independent Councilor. From a very green beginning I have learned a good deal, and become interested and informed on a score of subjects about which I had not hitherto even thought much. It is absorbing, interesting, demanding, invigorating, testing, maddening, frustrating, hard work. It also gives me a chance to try to help people— other than my immediate family—with problems, and it has widened my vision of humanity enormously. I find that dealing daily with all sorts of difficulties in the town and neighborhood helps greatly in getting trials nearer home into perspective.

I also try always to find time to indulge my passion for music and the theater, and I am fortunate in living in an area which caters to many cultural interests. And each summer there is Lourdes—this is now the highlight of my year—which reunites me with Ampleforth friends, lay and religious. When I first visited the place as a day pilgrim in my youth, I vowed never to set foot there again, but now I am really one of the Lourdes "miracles" because I regard my visits as a sort of cure. I miss it when I am not there, and often return in prayer to that magical place, made so very special by the "beautiful lady" and the simple girl Bernadette, who through her steadfast faith and trust has inspired many thousands of suffering pilgrims to accept their trials, even to rejoice in them. As I pray, I can transport myself to the Grotto by the swiftly flowing riving Gave where the figure of Mary, the mother of God, stands so serenely in the candlelit darkness—not a tawdry sentimental image, but the mediatrix of all grace.

In 1975 I left my rather too large house in Cheltenham and, with the help of my sister, bought a more manageable one just a little way out in what used to be the village of Charlton Kings. I owe a great debt to Margot, my only sister, who gave up her own life to share with me the care of Susie and the upbringing of my granddaughter. She has been generous and unselfish for all the years since, and has made it possible for me to do many things both for myself and my family, which would otherwise have been impossible. Her support has meant much to me—another blessing, another reason for counting myself lucky.

And perhaps a last reason for trying to live successfully as a widow: the belief that it is life itself and not just its quality which is precious, and the knowledge that heaven is not merely some strange place in the clouds, but somewhere *real*—the place from whence we came and where we return in the fullness of time. The fullness is the abundant life which Christ died to provide for us, and when we give our loved ones back to God we are letting them go into that peace which St. Paul says surpasses all understanding, and recommends as the glory which the eye has not seen, but which awaits the faithful children of God.

If I live as long as my own mother did, it is possible that all the joys of my widowhood—my remaining children—may be taken from me before I myself come to die. It is not a prospect which one can view with much of the calmness, courage, or wisdom of which I have so glibly spoken. But I shall still have hope. I shall still be attached to the Lord through the working of the Holy Spirit and the beneficence of his gifts, if only I can go on trying to use them.

When Susie died a friend wrote to me, "the first of your children to arrive safely," and this thought, so aptly put, has sustained me and will do so through the dark sad days which inevitably lie ahead. That wonderful great English saint, Thomas More, had a lovely prayer which I must try to say more and more: "Thank you dear Jesus for all you have given me, for all you have taken from me, for all you have left me." Perhaps the secret is to try always to share what the Lord leaves us, and to listen to the Prophet Isaiah when he says that if we do, "Your light will shine like the dawn and your wound be quickly healed over. Your integrity will go before you and the glory of the Lord behind you. Cry, and the Lord will answer; call, and he will say, I am here" (Is. 58: 8-9).

I am fairly certain he will also say, "Do not be afraid. I have redeemed you. I have called you by your name; you are mine." I do feel I am his, and that because he has helped me so wonderfully so far, I can trust him forever, and I do. Although he has taken away my husband, one whole child, and half another, and even if he should leave me entirely alone, I hope I can try to be brave enough to join St. Thomas More and say, "Pray, that we may merrily meet in Heaven"—and truly believe it.

# Suddenly Single

*by Susan Wheeler*

In the summer of 1979 my husband Michael, my two daughters, twelve-year-old Sophie and nine-year-old Alexandra, and I spent four idyllic weeks in Greece. Imprinted deeply on my mind are some words I had written to my godmother: "Our holiday is perfect bliss. Love from the happiest girl in the world." That I remained for another two weeks.

On our return from Greece, we went immediately to Kent for our annual golf and bucket and spade holiday. Shortly after this we attended Mass together at Downside Abbey in Somerset for what was to be the last time. Michael confided to me after Mass that he had just thanked Jesus so much for me and for his wonderful children. "I am such a lucky man and I do not deserve you." During this past year our love for one another had grown so strong that I had become apprehensive and frightened—how could such a Utopia continue?

Two days later, Michael was a dying man.

It was on the return journey to London that the first symptoms of illness manifested themselves. We were traveling back in two cars which always caused great excitement with the girls because, although we started together, I would always arrive at least half an hour after Michael. On this occasion, as I drove up to the house the girls rushed out to me and said, "Daddy has had two accidents." I did not pay much attention and was faintly amused.

The following day he had another near accident returning from his golf club. So when in the late evening of the same day he said that something most strange had just happened in his head, I immediately rang our G.P. who assured me it was neither a stroke nor a heart attack but that he should go to the eye specialist. The specialist saw him late the next day and said his eyes were perfectly all right.

I began to see a change in Michael. He was bumping into things and people, and feeling tired. We visited the neurologist that same week. I met Michael at the hospital after his day at the office which, as it turned out, was his last day there. After a hectic round of doctors and medical establishments, we arrived home to the clamor of children.

Michael lay on his bed deeply worried, the children snuggled down beside him as was their wont, but he could no longer bear the pain that had now begun inside his head; so the children kissed him on each eye, on the nose and mouth, which was the ritual, and I put them to bed.

The next day we had an appointment for a brain scan and afterwards we were to go on to another hospital where there was a bed ready for him. As Michael sat in the garden until it was time to go, an old friend from the USA unexpectedly visited us and talked to him while I made frantic phone calls to family, friends, and office. I learned several years later that Michael divulged to her his terrible worry about his illness. He did not want to tell me his worst fears, and he told her that he loved me so much and did not want to die.

We first drove the children to our friends, the Browns, and then went on to the hospital for the scan. After the scan I found that I had to lift Michael's legs into the car. We got hopelessly lost looking for the clinic where he was to stay overnight, in spite of knowing exactly where it was.

We were both in a state of shock at Michael's condition, which I could see deteriorating second by second. He had become slightly lopsided and was forgetting very simple things—totally out of character.

Michael insisted on carrying his suitcase from the car. When we arrived at his room on the fourth floor, he entered and immediately collapsed, turning blue. That night as I left his room, the matron, who was standing behind me, put her hands on my shoulders. I can feel them now—very heavy and strong. She said, "Prepare yourself, Mrs. Wheeler, you are going to need all the strength you have." That was the first moment of reality. The day had moved with such speed that I had had no time to think of anything but the urgency of each moment.

The next day the neurologist told me that Michael might not live more than a few hours. However, he made it through the night, but was now paralyzed and his sight was partially affected. A brain tumor was diagnosed and it was decided that a biopsy should be performed.

The neurologist wanted me to tell Michael that he was going to die soon, but I resisted; he was still in great shock and I wanted to protect him and give him hope. I felt that if I simply said "You are going to die," he would not fight or have any hope at all.

Sophie was due to go to her new boarding school the same day Michael was to have his biposy—not a good combination of events. Fortunately I had already packed her trunk and most of the other details were out of the way. I took her to the clinic to see Michael the day she was to go to school and we drove in an ambulance with him to the hospital where he was to have another scan. This was, of course, exciting and fun for her.

The emotions I felt in being torn between staying with

Michael and taking Sophie to school were overwhelming. I was trying to give my love and attention to both of them. While I had my two girls to think of, my overriding priority was to be always with Michael. He was miserable if I left him even for a few minutes; he always questioned why I had been gone so long.

Without the wonderful support and assistance of friends I could not have faced this difficult situation. My brother and friends drove Sophie and me down to school where I made the necessary arrangements for her, and then they rushed me back to see Michael just as he was about to be sedated for his biopsy. I was able to tell him that I had left Sophie happy. I gave him a kiss, and then, from the emotional strain of it all, promptly fainted.

The biopsy showed that the tumor was too advanced for surgery, so this was the beginning of a two-month stay in the clinic. However, that night I was told again that he might only live for another few hours. My feeling of desperation was so great that I was now prepared to do anything to help Michael—from black magic onwards.

Knowing of my feelings, my friends, the Browns, drove through the night to get in touch with a medium whom they knew. They brought her a photograph of Michael which was needed for the "treatment." The medium knew he was very ill but felt that she could make him better—although she could not restore him to his former health. However, she said she could help him only if he was free from the interference of the cobalt treatment. I had to make the decision at this point between putting my faith in the healer or continuing with the doctors and their medication.

I chose the medics—rightly or wrongly I shall never know. I did pray desperately to particular saints at this time, willing a voice to say "Do this." I was advised by friends to alert my solicitor, to change my separate account to Michael's bank and to organize power of attorney. All these items were of enormous importance. It was only thanks to my diligent friends that nothing was overlooked.

During the days of high crisis, Michael's friends overwhelmed me with their continuous visitations and their support in so many ways. I did not feel alone because the feeling of togetherness with them was so strong. After two weeks of intense pain, continuous ice packs on his head, and unconsciousness, Michael made an unexpected recovery. At that time he had twenty to thirty visitors a week, and sometimes that many in a day. In fact, life began to get quite out of hand, particularly as everyone who came seemed to come armed with champagne. With the daily help of his secretary we finally had to organize an appointment system.

Although Michael was still very much in control and wanted his letters written and decisions carried through, I suddenly realized that I was being expected to make decisions that he would normally have made without much thought. He no longer had the ability to work out anything complicated. This was another step in my own growing up: I was suddenly on my own without a navigator in seas that I did not know, but were familiar to Michael. This was my first taste of isolation even though I was still with him.

It is worth remembering that the awfulness of isolation only comes on those who have enjoyed company. When a wife is facing the coming death of her husband this freezing sensation is already creeping up on her.

Alexandra arrived each afternoon after school, and Sophie came home each weekend to see her father. My day would start by driving Alexandra to school and then going immediately to the clinic to arrive at half past eight. Very often Michael already had a visitor with him. I would stay until he was either asleep or peaceful, between nine and twelve at night. I then had a ten minute drive to the Browns where Alexandra and I stayed for seven weeks. Each evening they had a delicious dinner prepared and waiting for me. Their love and support and closeness is beyond description. Day after day, night after night, I felt I was going mad and doubted my own ability to make decisions, but with the constant love and friendship and selflessness of my own family and precious friends, I remained reasonably sane.

All through Michael's illness and in the five years since his death, I have had two particular girl friends who, together with my brothers, were always there, helping me with advice and decisions of everyday life.

For those who have anything to do with the bereaved I cannot put strong enough emphasis on the value of friends. They can be old friends or complete strangers, but I have concluded, not only as the result of my own experience but also through my experience as a bereavement counselor, that many people end up needing mental treatment of one sort or another, which in my opinion could have been avoided by good, continuous counseling from family and friends. The importance of this counseling lies in being with the bereaved during the time of illness and trauma, and then continuing afterwards to keep in touch, and listening, during the progression of the years, to the numerous worries that evolve.

Whether or not I was prepared for Michael's death I do not really know. I was told on two separate occasions that he would die immediately and he did not. I only thought in terms of him getting better, never of dying. There was no room in my mind for such thoughts. Having made a remarkable recovery, he was dressed each day and sat in a chair and the medics decided he could go home. I felt we were over the first hurdle.

We took a hospital bed home and arranged a rotation of day and night nurses, and his physiotherapist was to start his day at half past seven in the morning. We also bought a very necessary wheelchair, so that he could be moved from room to room.

I worried continuously when and how I should tell the children their father was going to die. I finally told them one evening when Michael was now in a coma. We had just collected Sophie from boarding school. It was dark, my brother was driving, and the children and I were sitting in the back seat of the car. The girls had jumped into the car, full of chatter, Sophie saying "I must tell Daddy I have..." That was my cue. I remember holding them very tightly while I told them. Their immediate reply was "You're going to be a widow"; "You're so young"; "We won't be able to go to Disney World." None of their remarks made any impression on me at the time, but now, of course, they have become central to my life and I find them poignant— "Out of the mouths of babes and sucklings."

We arrived home forty minutes later. The girls rushed into Michael's room and lay down beside him with their arms around him. Over the following few days we would talk to him and sit with him, the girls asking many medical questions which happily were dealt with by the nurses.

Why does one hesitate to tell the children in the first place? It may be that you feel you are protecting them from certain trauma and you have the awful fear that you will not be strong enough to sustain and support them because of your own weak situation. But I am certain you should tell them the truth before their father dies, if at all possible. If it is a long process you can more easily prepare the way. To a very small degree I did try to prepare them with a prayer they had always said in their night prayers: "Must Jesus bear His cross alone and all the world go free? No, there's a cross for everyone and there's a cross for me." This prayer helped me over the weeks to explain to them that sometimes we would be very unhappy.

The decision to tell Michael he was going to die was even more difficult than telling the children. I felt like a hypocrite at having put up a front for so long, pretending that I was confident he would get better and letting him talk about what he would do when he was well.

Looking back, one can question this subterfuge: did I let him down by not telling him sooner? Did I help him by keeping him in ignorance and a false peace? I did not have total confidence in myself. If I had, there would have been no dilemma. As things turned out, our G.P. finally told him, because the moment arrived, and he could not, and should not, have evaded it.

Maybe I should have told Michael sooner, but when dealing with a loved one you feel a natural instinct to protect him. I now believe strongly that you should always tell someone they are going to die, unless, of course, it is known that they would rather not be told.

Michael was crushed and deeply depressed and wanted me by his side all the time. I can remember holding his hands and willing my life into his body. To come face to face with each other, both knowing the truth, was unbearable. We were so afraid for each other's feelings, trying to control overwhelming emotion. The world stopped, our minds stopped, we could not touch each other. The moment of crisis had come and gone, but it remained with us.

Fortunately we had a marvelous parish priest who was perfect for Michael both spiritually and intellectually. He was an immense solace and help to Michael, who, in spite of his tremendously strong faith and conviction, suffered most terribly in coming to terms with dying. He gradually became reconciled and peaceful but he never wanted to die. "If Jesus wants me I will go—don't be sad," he constantly repeated.

Michael's attitude has been my motivation, I think. If he could make the supreme effort to become reconciled with death, I can become resigned to building a positive and full life again.

Michael had a wonderful relationship with his nurses and in his better days the hilarity and laughter that went on between them was a tonic to me. Very often when I woke in the morning I would hear hysterical laughter coming from Michael's room which was beneath me and I would know his physiotherapists had arrived. This warmed my heart and I felt such gratitude that he liked them so much and vice versa. People tell me that we did have a wonderful atmosphere of gentle humor and love that seemed to permeate the house. Michael himself exuded great strength and peace and endless dry humor.

It was providential that on the evening Michael went into his final coma the parish priest arrived unexpectedly to give us Communion. He also heard Michael's confession on this his last night of consciousness. I remember waking that night and seeing the vision of Michael's face looking up at me, translucent. I remember thinking he must need me and I wanted to get up to go to him. But the next thing I knew it was morning. I got out of bed and rushed downstairs to find that he had had a distressing night with intense pain in his head and he was now in a coma. I was very upset because the nurse had not called me, but she had thought that I would be too distressed at Michael's condition. I felt, however, that she should have realized that what was important was my being there to support him. It is quite common to make the mistake of trying to help the living at the expense of the dying.

I learned that although a patient may be in a coma, he can still understand what is being said. He can experience deep loneliness and fear in this state. I held Michael's hand all day during this last week of coma, and talked, reassuring him that I would be all right without him. The girls came in at intervals and lay beside him.

*   *   *

After Michael's death I was no exception in feeling the extraordinary tiredness that envelopes one's whole being: terrible sleeping patterns, depressions, incessant crying. Sleep became priority number one. I no longer knew this crumpled, unpredictable, forgetful, disoriented, and indecisive creature I had become. I want to tell every widow that you have to get to know this new person which is yourself.

Gradually, in the first year, I started to do as many things as I could fit into the day—along with plenty of sleep. First, I took up picture framing. This was a disaster because I was always so exhausted. On one occasion I disgraced myself by falling asleep on the work bench and practically poking out the eye of the tutor with a six-foot piece of wood that I seemed to have absolutely no control over.

After that, I joined a book club that met once a month. There were a lot of new faces there, and I was encouraged to read. Next, I took classes at the Royal School of Needlework in gold thread work, an ancient craft that had always fascinated me. I found this tremendously therapeutic. Encouraging some metal thread to turn a corner, stabbing my finger with a viciously sharp needle, I was engrossed for an entire day once a week. This creative occupation relaxed my mind, I was anonymous, and I did not have to speak! I then joined a silversmith class and took great pleasure in making rings and bracelets for my daughters.

In the third year after Michael's death I took up French conversation which I did privately. Again it required great mental effort and I think it made my mind stronger and my French better. I next went to the London School of Bridge and met some very nice people. Many, many times I felt like running out of the door during the lessons, but I did achieve the Intermediate class!

These all helped in their different ways, but initially I had to make a superhuman effort to take them up, to "get them on the road." I was always making excuses for not going. I was helped in this, as in so much else, by the encouragement of friends who were already involved in these activities and who introduced me to them.

My husband's company employed me intermittently— and still does—to help them organize business dinners and receptions. Meeting my husband's clients with a different hat on was very disturbing initially, but because I had so enjoyed my very full business life with my husband, I was determined to try to see if I could sustain this new life in his work environment. Friends urged me not to continue, but I have, and because of it I have continued to see many faces, and preserve friendships with people who were essentially Michael's business friends. This has helped the isolation factor enormously and I would suggest caution to any widow who decides to throw everything and everyone to the four winds and start again in unknown waters.

There are many devastating comments made by one's greatest friends or by total strangers, which, in the early days of widowhood, have a totally disorienting effect on one because the mental shock has been too great to control. In fact, I used to find, and still do to a lesser degree, that it was like receiving an electric shock through my entire body. "You're so young" became one of the most disturbing phrases for me to contend with because it reminded me of the horror of being young and having "my whole life ahead of me," and now having to face it alone. I have a deep yearning to be old today, and not tomorrow. The accepted concept of youth is something wonderful that offers hope and future, but to the young new widow it really feels like salt being poured on a wound.

The way to grapple with this is to be conscious that such remarks are innocent and are intended to be comforting, and are said by people who are distressed at your distress. It is only when you have had several of these encounters that you can begin to cope with them, and this is then another step on the way to achieving a new wholeness.

There is no progress through bitterness. There must be mental resignation to one's state. Bitterness excludes people and your world closes in. With resignation you can go out again to people and this enables them to come in to you, but they need the encouragement from you, the widow, to mention your dead husband, for instance. For they, the unbereaved, are hesitant and unsure in this world of grief.

I do remember that for about a year I met so many people who were suffereing for one reason or another: recovering from breakdowns, heart attacks, recently divorced, spouse disappeared, fellow widows, or just unhappily married. It did open my eyes to the world, but I also found it overwhelming at that time because of my own weak and vulnerable state and it had an adverse effect on me. Not only did I feel my life was finished and that I was on the heap of rejects, but I felt I would no longer be treated like an ordinary healthy person. I was a different person—but who? It was as though I had missed a generation and had taken on the role of grandmother.

With hindsight, meeting these suffering people did things for me. First I saw that I was not the only miserable being, and secondly it encouraged me to handle myself in a positive manner. I would describe the way I set about it as a "big act." Everyday was another day on the stage—the same story but a different scene. I had to re-assert, re-orientate, and strengthen myself—which brings me to another well-worn phrase used erroneously to give encouragement to the bereaved: "Time will heal."

"Time" for me has been a long, black tunnel—so long perhaps that it has no end. It is in this tunnel that I have to find a new light. That light has to be strong, sustaining, and everlasting. Everlasting because it has to guide me beyond the end of the tunnel to an eternity. As a bereaved person you do not want time to pass because time distances you from the one you have loved, and that is painful. But in order to achieve a new life this has to be faced, as is so clearly set out by Dr. Murray Parkes in his book *Bereavement*. He describes time as

> the gradual withdrawal of interest and loyalty from the dead person and the final achieving of freedom to make emotional and intellectual investments in the world. . . . A psycho-social transition in which we re-assess our picture of the world and our means of being a part of it. . . . Readjustment first to an environment in which the deceased is missing, and then in which he is absent.

Recently, I have become a bereavement counselor at St.

Joseph's Hospice in Hackney. This bereavement counseling is a new venture: I train groups of eight to ten people at a time, who then counsel the family and friends of those who have died in the care of the Hospice, where terminally sick people come specifically to die. This counseling has been immensely rewarding for me and almost a relief to know that I can give comfort in some small way. Two of the many observations I have made from the work are that everyone is unique, and that it appears to me younger widows have a different set of emotions to deal with than older widows.

This partly comes about by the way one is treated, but also because, by the natural cycle of life, the young widow is, mentally, completely unprepared for the death of her spouse. Whatever the reason for death, I feel that the younger widow has an immense additional burden by the very nature of life. This does not mean I in any way minimize bereavement in later life—to each individual this loss is unique. Each part of one's life is a preparation for what is to come and then a development of what has gone before.

> We meet, we relate, we separate. Parting is the price of meeting. Such is the pattern of life until we do not meet again—this is death. And if we still break and meet again but do not relate, this too is a kind of death.
>
> (Jean Charnley, *The Art of Child Placement*)

Within this structure certain things happen: the progression from childhood to adulthood, falling in love, marriage, children; and the cycle continues with grandchildren, retirement, and eventually the dignity and wisdom of old age and, inevitably, death. But there is an additionally acute pain if this separation occurs in a young life—it is happening before its natural time. The sap which is rising, the adrenalin which is flowing with the excitement and challenge of each new day, is inexplicably extinguished. I quote from *Separation*, by Jessie Taft:

> But the fact remains that human beings are not passive victims of trauma from birth to death. They do find fulfillment in experiences that are hard to leave. They can overcome the traumatic aspects of painful parting by the discovery of unused strength for living in the self. True, man is a suffering being, but he is also a powerful, creative force, with a capacity for moulding the outside world into something he can also claim as his own. What man resists above all is internal interference with any phase of his living before he is ready to abandon it. It is not the leaving but the lack of control over the leaving that he fears. If he can possess to some degree the ending phase of even the deepest relationship, so that he feels as part of himself the movement towards the new, then he cannot only bear the growth process however painful, but he can accept it with *positive affirmation*.
>
> In any separation there is a wound. But it can be treated in such a way that it will leave only a little scar.

This wound needs very special attention.

In spite of one's own emotional weaknesses one must turn one's attention to the children: they in some ways can be even more deprived, can need as much dialogue over their loss, and have even less opportunity to express it, and so need to be encouraged to talk.

For me at first it always produced a breakdown of tears to mention Michael with the girls, but now we can laugh and joke and have long, long discussions because all their own early lives can only live through my memory, and it is right that they should gain this from me.

At his funeral Mass, both children composed a farewell prayer, and I feel that Sophie put her suffering into the context of Our Lord's life when she wrote: "Dear Jesus, I thank you for all that you have done to make us happy. For having come into this world to save me, for being a little child like me, for being cold and hungry often, for being scourged at the pillar, and being crowned with thorns and nailed to the hard wood of the cross, for having died for me on the cross and risen again, and gone to heaven to get a place ready for me."

And Alexandra's plea for courage and help has been answered: "Dear Jesus, I thank you for taking Daddy to heaven in such a peaceful way. Help us to help others when they need courage, as our friends have helped us. Amen."

# Tomorrow Be Today

*by Maire Tugendhat*

All things must change
To something new, to something strange:
Nothing that is can pause or stay,
The moon will wax, the moon will wane,
The mist and cloud will turn to rain,
The rain and mist to cloud again,
Tomorrow be today.

Longfellow

*      *      *

The Master is come, and calleth for thee.

John 11:28

Dearest Diana,

How nice to hear from you after so long, and thank you so much for your letter. By chance and despite your uncertainty, it reached me at exactly the right time. It was tonight two years ago that I sent for the doctor, and later, in the small hours, that he died. Naturally it has been in my mind all day and was my first thought on awakening. Two short years ago, yet sometimes now instantly present and still happening; at other times far away and small as something seen through the corridors of time.

You know it all, though. That dread angel also swept

through your doors two years ago—all but two months before he passed through ours. And almost without warning in each case. He came, he beckoned, he left, and we were alone. Still surrounded by the same people, the same things, the same sounds, yet as alone as if adrift on a polar floe.

No one can understand this until it overtakes them. One can read about it, hear about it, think about it, but one simply cannot imagine what it is really like.

It is for this reason that I can never properly thank you, except in prayer, for the strength and support you gave me at the time.

As always,

M.

\*         \*         \*

Dearest Diana,

I loved hearing from you. Yes, of course you are right, and there are many more external aspects of grief than the ones of which I was writing. There can be, as in my case, the almost anesthetizing effect of shock during the first week or ten days after the death, punctuated by stabbing cramps and pains, and a total inability to cry. For me, it was not until after the funeral that the loss was fully felt. And then, during those following days it was wretched to be alone, particularly at night. Yet what can one's friends do unless they are already living in the house?

One needs to have friends nearby for support, yet at the same time, I myself could not have borne condolers. I think people must realize that the bereaved do not want over-sentimentality or emotionalism, but need, above every-thing, tenderness. They also need firmness, but firmness lovingly administered. Their defenses are down and their emotions are bare. The earth is stopped and there is no refuge. They cannot acknowledge or fully believe their loss. This is no time for friends to be diffident. If we want to strengthen, encourage, and reinforce a totally dis-oriented spirit, we must give what is warm and alive in ourselves, however undemonstrative we may normally be. A clasp around the shoulders and a firm strong hug will go further than words when someone is too dazed to care. It may even provoke an outburst of tears which, if allowed to flow, may bring unutterable relief and relax those knots and cramps brought on by the inability to cry. Perhaps you don't remember, but I remember well how you held my coat collar tight up under my chin and gave me an affec-tionate shake while you smiled at me. It is things like that warm physical contact in a world of interior ice that are literally lifesavers.

But in the long run, the only thing to do is to will oneself back; to begin, as soon as one feels the slightest return of life, reassembling one's days and finding and following an occupation that requires one's full attention and endeavor. And this two-way therapy is what I was writing about in my last letter. By this time realization has probably hit full on target and the previous numbness been replaced by hideous depression which makes it even more urgent to force one's thoughts and actions into an external channel. To start with, there are the necessary papers and business matters to be dealt with. But in this connection, I feel it is essential to postpone the making of any important deci-sions or the taking of any irrevocable steps.

Of course for many people the simple mechanics of these

everyday matters are a desperate problem. You, Diana, are practical and competent and have always managed your own affairs; but, had I not my tirelessly kind and devoted children, I do not know what I should have done. To be able to help and advise people in practical ways is to be a tower of strength indeed. It will perhaps also save the newly widowed a lot of unnecessary expense as they would otherwise have to get professional advice for every smallest thing.

Then there is the question of loneliness. I have found that after awhile—particularly for women—invitations decline, and unless the widow is careful, this is aggravated by the tendency to refuse them in the early weeks because she lacks the spirit to go out and be gay. This may change, though, after four or five months, and the widow may now *need* to be asked and want to take her place again at people's tables. At this time her friends should make a point of drawing her into their circle.

After the death of a spouse, it seems that the normal habit of living and moving in mixed company comes to an end. Suddenly, one's own sex predominates—as equally for men in their clubs or quiet pubs as for women with their ladies' lunches or tea-parties.

And as you and I have found, Diana, after the pressure and bustle of a full family life, we no longer even hear the sound of voices in an adjacent room or the banging of doors and quick feet on the stairs. In fact, after two silent years we still unconsciously live in an attitude of waiting—waiting for him to come home, or for the telephone to ring to explain why he doesn't. It will pass of course, in time, but forty years is not wiped out in two, and that is what we have to live with now.

You know Siegfried Sassoon's lovely sonnet beginning,

"When I'm alone." Have you read it lately? I always loved it, and even thought I understood it. Now I really do understand it. In case you have not got it handy, here it is.

"When I'm alone"—the words tripped off his tongue
As though to be alone were nothing strange.
"When I was young," he said; "when I was young..."
I thought of age, and loneliness, and change.
I thought how strange we grow when we're alone,
And how unlike the selves that meet and talk,
And blow the candles out and say good-night.
Alone...the word is life endured and known.
It is the stillness where our spirits walk
And all but inmost faith is overthrown.

Take care of yourself,

M.

\*      \*      \*

Dearest Diana,

I agree with you entirely. There is so much to say, to discuss, to ponder; and scarcely anyone with whom one is able to do it. The scythe has cut our swath and we remain stubble without a flower. We feel, some of us gratefully, that this is the countdown to death. Personally, I do not feel this. I remember the way mown grass rises and thickens until it affords more pasture than before for the cattle to pull and the sheep to nibble. Our neighbors and friends may not care to be thought of as cows or rams, but most of them in our position would be glad of some extra grazing!

It is, I am convinced, the greatest mistake to turn our faces away, to count ourselves out, to refuse involvement of any sort because our own lives have been shattered. You and I have arrived at the tea-time of life—five o'clock shall we say—and the shadows stretch before us, but there is plenty of daylight left. It would be a pity to sit in the darkness of our self-centeredness while there is still so much we can do before "the night cometh when no man can work." I don't say we should go out and make nuisances of ourselves, but we should leave our doors on the latch and answer every knock. Those are terrifying words in the parable: "Thou fool, this night shall thy soul be required of thee," because when that moment comes we shall have had our chance.

But not everybody fears to go on alone and longs to die. Some just drift into the next world, as the lady whose memorial tablet in Bath Abbey says:

> ...and she,
> To live without him tried,
> But liked it not, and died.

Many are haunted by dread of that day which each new page of the calendar brings nearer. I can think now of two or three who have confessed as much to me. One, a nun in her early middle age, said, "I am terrified of dying. Not of death, but of dying." And another, a woman who had suddenly been taken ill, said, "I might die...I might *die!*" Of course she might. And certainly one day she will.

This characteristic of bereavement and grief, this longing to leave a world that has lost its center for us, this terror of the beast that will spring we know not when, this *fear*, will engulf us too unless, enfeebled as we are by the total collapse of life as we know it, we make a stupendous, even a heroic effort. The poor ostrich puts his head in the sand and stays there. But the swan, after scrambling to get airborne flies free. Let us, you and I, be swans! The whole of what remains to us of life will not be long enough for us to get over our loss, but we are used to giving affection and solace, and to listening patiently and trying to untangle troubles. We can and should go on doing this in gratitude for what we have had.

Years ago, but as clear as yesterday in my memory, I had the most wonderful dream. No doubt, like all dreams, it was led up to by events that had gone before—in this case a dance and a long drive home in the dawn, and falling into bed at about four o'clock in the morning. In my dream I was looking at a sturdy male shoulder clothed in a navy blue suit. The right shoulder. That is all it was, but I was filled with confidence. Here was the rock of ages as far as I was concerned. I suppose I was nineteen or twenty at the time and no doubt in some sort of mental or spiritual wobble. But when I see people unhappy, disappointed or afraid, and they are all about us unconsciously giving themselves away, I recall that shoulder and the strength it symbolized. Men and women of all ages—but I am beginning to think particularly in the later ages—need shoulders to weep on and bosoms against which to lean, even to sob, if they have to. Men perhaps more than women, because they seem to find it increasingly difficult to make new friends as they get older. E. P. Hartley put this very clearly in *The Will and the Way*. He says:

> It happens to many people who have passed the normal span that they lose the capacity for many forms of enjoyment, and not least for friendship. Even if they still have the capacity, death has deprived them of most of their friends, and how can they make new friends when time is so short and it is too late to create the background of shared experience on which the stability of friendship depends.

Old ladies are better at making, and keeping, new friends

than men are. With them the interest, the excitement of novelty in the form of another person does not so quickly die down. Needless to say why: for them, life is a process of discovery and rediscovery in the field of human relationships, of which they never tire, whereas men tend to withdraw into themselves and look backwards to their past amorous and business achievements rather than to the present or to the future, where no such prospects of personal or financial expansion lie. And sometimes, as old people will, they become critical and even turn against those who have been nearest and dearest to them.

Well, we are women, so let us light our fires in the falling dusk, feeding them with everything we can salvage from our own happy lives—and we have both been unusually blessed by love and kindness all our days—and the glow will draw people in from the dark to share the warmth and help keep the beasts of prey outside the ring of light.

This letter is longer than I meant it to be, but writing these things helps to clear my mind. Perhaps you will dispute parts of it! Write when you can, I would love to have your views. We would never be able to talk in this way, too many irrelevancies would keep getting in.

As ever,

M.

*     *     *

Dearest Diana,

Thank you for your letter. This question of belief or disbelief, all these doubts and uncertainties.... This feeling that we have built our houses upon sand, and that, now that the props and stays of our existence have been withdrawn, we are sinking into the unknown—I am sure it shatters the peace of mind of hundreds. And those whom it torments are in most cases those who do not know where to turn for comfort. To whom could I write about it if not to you? And to whom could you come if not to me? We do not know if our other friends suffer from it. People seldom speak of these things freely.

I believe it is another side-effect of shock following the death of a spouse. These side-effects persist, or even develop months after a widow appears to have regained normal stability. We may think the worst is over and that we are able to take our place again in life, but the tenuous balance can be upset again in a trice. In can take years to rebuild the breached walls of the spirit. Disbelief can be the direct consequence of the annihilating quality of grief, which sometimes leaves no defense against the sense of utter loss and disillusionment.

If we feel this way, we must force ourselves to cast off into total darkness and steer by will alone. The catechism taught us that the three powers of the soul are the memory, the understanding, and the will. In this crisis the memory may have little to offer, the understanding may be paralyzed, and only the will remains. So we must simply repeat over and over: "I don't believe, but I *will* to be-lieve...I don't love, but I *will* to love..." We must recite the Creed with our whole *will*. Everything we need is there, including the triumphant and consoling: "I *believe* in the resurrection of the dead, and the life of the world to come."

Speaking of trying to navigate in a world which seems to have temporarily lost all its meaning; in your letter you also mentioned prayer, and how difficult even that can be, whether or not it came easily before. It is the only refuge, but how hard to believe it is being heard! In that connection, I must tell you a true story about my mother that happened when she was utterly shattered by the telegram announcing that my father had been killed in the Great War, in May 1915. They had been married for only five years. In her desolation she longed for some tangible sign that he was still near her, and begged that someone would, that day, bring her one single flower. That afternoon, when we children were going out with our nurse—we were five and three years old—I saw an arum lily lying in the road. I ran to pick it up and took it back into the house where I put it in my mother's hands. She told me the story thinking I would have forgotten the incident but I remember it vividly.

Prayer, for people who have forgotten how to pray, or never learned to, perhaps sounds too strange and difficult to attempt. If only they realized how natural and easy it is—just talking to the Almighty as I am talking to you. As an example of the sadness of people thinking they can't pray, here is one more story. One night, six or seven years ago, I was awakened by the telephone. The caller was a stranger—an extremely desperate man who had been told that day that his wife was terminally ill, and he was to take her home from the hospital the following day. He had, in his wretchedness and his need to talk, picked up the phone and dialed at random. He and his wife had two children. "What shall I tell them?" he kept saying. We talked for a long time, in the course of which he said he knew no clergyman, never went to church, and had no idea how to pray. At the end he implored: "Promise me you'll pray for me." I keep my promise daily, for him, his children, and his wife. Episodes like that bring home sharply the terrible unhappiness this state of loss creates.

You are always in my mind, Diana, but now you are on it as well. We will keep each other, and those many others, company in this long cold vigil. "Faith is a supernatural gift of God,"—the catechism again!—but we have lost it, mislaid it in the recent tumult. But if we hold out our hands it will be restored to us. And as the Welsh hymn has it, we can say:

Hear us, O Lord, Thy sea is so large,
And our boat is so small.

Ever and always,

M.

\*         \*         \*

When thou passeth through the water I will be with thee,
and through the rivers, they shall not overthrow thee.

Isaiah 53:2

Dearest Diana,

You write of loneliness. That is probably the biggest problem for people in our situation—and for practically every other person who leads a single life. There are so many reasons why, like it or not, people of all ages must live alone. But I think we must consider those others separately—do not let us forget to discuss this. For the moment, however, it is our own plight that we are trying to clarify and accept.

It is not only the loneliness, it is that perpetual prick of remorse that haunts us too. "Why was I so impatient that day?" "Why didn't I help even though I was tired?" "Why," and "If only..." It is no use, the milk is spilt. We are not angels, and those were our less admirable moments. For our comfort, don't you think they were outweighed by our better ones, and that, as far as we could, we only lived for our loves? Now they are gone before us and sleep the sleep of peace, and that is best for them. But we are left alone, and how we miss them, consciously and unconsciously, all the time. One corner of our minds has become a recording machine whispering, "That lovely day we were here together and I lost my glove..." or, "He'd have liked this man," or, "This woman's wit would have really appealed to him."

An aunt of mine—now well into her eighties—who lost her husband in a flu epidemic forty years ago, said to me, "You never stop missing." Forty years of missing!

Never stop missing—how hopeless it sounds until you think about it from another angle. Just by missing him you are bringing him to you, he is in your memory and your mind, he is with you. If you could forget him and be happy he would not be there. While you long for him he is at your side and you can even speak to him, mind to mind, "Darling, stay with me." Or as I once did, right at the beginning, aloud in the street, "Darling, give me your hand." You feel utterly lost, away out on the coldest star in space, but you can speak to him as easily as you did when you said, "The marmalade, please," at breakfast. I have only just realized this, and for the moment at least, it is a great comfort. But no consolation is permanent. Our moods are always in flux, largely at the mercy of our health. We have a cold, or a strained wrist, and the blackness is upon us again. So we

must meet it objectively and practically. We are still bound
by this body, still held by gravity to this globe, still

> Rolled round in earth's diurnal course
> With rocks and stones and trees.
>> (Wordsworth, *A Slumber did my Spirit Seal*)

This for the moment is our world in which we still have
our passage to work, so in the words of the song, "Whatever the weather, we'll weather the weather, whether we
like it or not."

Have you ever discussed the subject of loneliness with
anyone much further along the road than you and I, someone with whom it has become a way of life, as it were? Not
long ago I spent two or three hours with a friend I had not
seen for several years. Her husband died sixteen years ago
and they were devoted to one another. She is a very musical person, and wrote many books on music. Her beautiful,
inlaid mahogany piano stood closed with papers and maga-
zines in orderly piles on top, together with the tray from
which she had given me a drink. I asked, "Don't you ever
play now?" She answered, "I haven't touched the keys
since Martin died." How sad that is, and what a pity. Soon
afterwards she said an interesting thing in reply to my
question as to whom, among our mutual friends, had been
her greatest support in the months and years following her
husband's death. She answered at once, "The Smiths. For a
long time I thought it was *she*, but now I realize it was *he*."

It is that kind of support I had in mind in my last letter,
when I said we should not lock ourselves into our own
souls, or words to that effect. I have always been certain—
now more than ever—that one should never withhold
anything one can give. A closed face, instead of a smile, can
sometimes put the finishing touch to misery. It was the
most amazing thing—I even thought it was miraculous—

how the first time I went out after G's death every soul I met, and I really believe *every* soul, smiled at me, and those I had to speak to answered warmly and with kindness in their eyes. Needless to say I've met the scowlers since, and the stony-eyed, all on their way to nowhere, each in his own desert. But that warmth at exactly the right moment shines like a rainbow in my memory.

Do write soon if you can,

M.

*　　　*　　　*

Dearest Diana,

A lovely full letter to thank you for, all crammed with pen pictures of people and things! And now you are alone, you say, and hating it. No voice, except the potted voices of radio and television, to break the long hours of silence. I know exactly what you mean, do believe me. But neither you nor I are so alone as all those countless others, young and old, rich and poor, who live by themselves and truly have no one in the world to turn to for friendship and support. The loneliness all about us is formidable and terrifying, and worst of all, is often undiscoverable. But you are not talking about this sort of loneliness, nor the loneliness of Gethsemane—stripped to the kernel of the soul so that others might be saved. You mean the physical and mental loneliness that follows when your husband has been taken and you have been left, with the air chill at your side. I mention the other two forms, among so many others, just to help myself as well as you to get things into perspective.

Do not forget that there is a sense in which we all, and always, walk alone. In our selfhood we are more solitary than the shadowy fox out on the frozen hill. Within and within and within ourselves, there is the essential "I" that entered the world alone and will leave it unaccompanied by any of those who have touched our lives as we passed through this world. And then alone we shall stand before the throne of God.

But that is the only sense in which we are really and utterly alone. And even there, as we are Christians, we know that we shall be supported by the prayers and spirits of those who have gone before us and those we have left behind, since we are all one in the communion of saints, heaven, earth, and purgatory.

So, if we think again of the loneliness you really mean, we are not so alone after all. Indeed, were we not sometimes by ourselves we would have no time to think, to evaluate, to come to terms with our inner selves. Do you not remember, as I certainly do, how in the midst of the daily pressures and demands of a full family life, you sometimes longed for an hour or two away from it all, and stole off on a solitary walk in the woods or fields simply to *be* alone? Away from the telephone, and the necessity of meeting someone, driving someone somewhere, welcoming someone, or scolding someone! It used to appear as though one half hour of peace would be the most wonderful thing in the world! And with several children, we used to be torn to pieces by this one's need for sympathy, that one's need for correction, that other one's need for encouragement, and so on. Now, alas, neither of us is any longer in danger of dementia from never having a moment to ourselves!

Somewhere I read that St. John of the Cross wrote:

Now guard I no flock, nor have I now other office.
For now my exercise is in loving alone.

He must have been old when he wrote that, but he meant to use his sunset years well, and if we are wise we will try to do the same. Now is the time to give all we have got to whoever will benefit by it, be it only for a moment in the exchange of a good-morning or a smile. One must live positively, be outgoing and giving. This is absolutely essential. We can at least see to it that our declining suns shed a warm sunset glow. You are very good at this, with the lovely knack of making everyone feel at home and wanted.

With love, as always,

M.

\*        \*        \*

Dearest Diana,

Thank you for your good advice and for urging me to go away. It is all very sound, but what an effort it requires even to get up and make a plan. It seems I drift into a routine without even realizing it.

Apropos to effort, how do you feel about party-going? I feel it is very nice of people to ask me, since many in our society think a single woman has very little party value outside her close friends and family. And so often no one takes any notice of her, which is why I hate to go to parties unaccompanied or without an anchor of some sort. Also, for some reason I feel frumpish and dull, even though I know that in the right company, among my friends and contemporaries, I am neither. Perhaps this is due to the theme of some gatherings—and especially if there is a large element of the go-getting young present who are well up on current events.

This feeling of insufficiency is not, of course, peculiar to widows like ourselves. It is even more marked in the case of divorced people, one of whom once told me that she had so often been looked through and "frozen-off" by the wives of men she had casually spoken to, that she preferred to avoid the occasions of these snubs. Others, on their own for whatever reason, see a wandering eye rest on them and then move on to something grander and more worthwhile. Obviously, this sort of cruel and inconsiderate behavior can only come from closed minds.

You remarked in one of your earliest letters that the flood of sympathy and good will after a death evaporates very quickly. People genuinely mean it when they offer condolences and invitations, but it comes too soon at first, and then life for them roars on and they completely forget about the widow. It is terribly important for friends to remain within reach for the first few months, and to continue to keep in touch long after: persuading the widow to a quiet supper or even a quiet drink; blowing the small flame until it is strong enough to hold its own in the reviving breath of life. We all ought to be aware of this, but of course we never are.

Thank you again for your urgings. I promise to think about it. Your own odyssey seems to have been a great success.

Always and ever,

M.

\*        \*        \*

I praise Thee while my days go on;
I love Thee while my days go on:
Through dark and dearth, through fire and frost,
With emptied arms and treasures lost,
I thank Thee while my days go on!

(Elizabeth Barrett Browning)

Dearest Diana,

Now that you are at home again and beginning to pick up the threads, has the contrast between the two states of living—the busy one and the very quiet one—made you wonder whether it is a good thing to live on your own? I have thought a lot about it, and am still thinking.

Last year a school-days friend told me that she was already making inquiries into the various possibilities offered by homes for the elderly against the time when she or her husband may need such a refuge. Another friend, a man who is involved in a charitable organization with exactly that aim, suggested that it might be financially a better idea if two, three, or four friends bought a house together, sharing the expenses and paying a housekeeper between them.

I remember saying to somebody once that it would soon be time to go to the poorhouse, and she replied, "How nice if we could all go to the same one!" One knows too, how many career women set up house together, though one does not always hear how it works out! Should it not, I suppose they can always return to their clubs or residential hotels if they can bring themselves to live alone again.

At our age, with visiting children, grandchildren, nephews, and nieces, it would not be practicable to actually live *à deux* unless we had an absurdly large house. But we could have different parts of the same house, with a front door and a side door, and inside, for convenience, a communicating door and an intercom. This would ensure privacy as well as companionship. According to our natures we can, to a greater or lesser degree, forego a certain amount of companionship, but it is very hard for anyone who has enjoyed the privilege of being able to withdraw from the crowd to once again live without privacy. At times we just have to be alone; otherwise we lose the point of balance within our souls without which our sense of purpose is shipwrecked, and we become neurotic and unreasonable. Such a state of affairs is death to any friendship. The poise and counterpoise of being together and being alone, of communication and of silence, leads to trust and emotional contentment. Tranquil and at ease in ourselves, we shall be the same with others, our friendship increasingly fruitful. If we forget, as far too many people do, that there is a secret garden within every person, the friendship will break down. Once individual separateness is lost communication is lost.

So for happy companionship we must agree to enjoy our solitary walks and secluded silences without hindrance. That said, we are free to steep ourselves in happy, tender, give-and-take togetherness, if we are fortunate enough to have such an opportunity.

Violet Asquith wrote: "Life is so short and death so certain, and when death comes the silence and separation are so complete, that one can never make too much of the ties and affections and relationships which bind us to the living." Nothing could be truer, and we must never forget it. If, in our old age and frailty, we opt for the solitary life, we may find ourselves falling back on the impersonal voice of the radio for company, and the ticking of the clock will replace the comfortable cough in the next room, or the sound of the outer door closing after entering feet.

Some will say that one should go and live with one's children, but I am not in favor of this. Life is difficult enough for them nowadays, and while one may sometimes be able to help them if needed, or even remain somewhat independent—seen but not heard so to speak—there will assuredly be a time (short of sudden death) when one will be more or less a burden. That is a sad word, so often heard on the lips of one's older friends and relations, "I do not want to be a burden." So, if at all possible, we shall want to spare our children.

That is as far as my thinking has gone. I am afraid that you may say it is very inconclusive, so I look forward to hearing your ideas.

> With love, as ever,
>
> M.

\*        \*        \*

Dearest Diana,

I am sorry not to have written for so long, apart from that quick card. But your letter was, as always, a great joy, and your remarks on personal relationships have given me much to think about. What a lot of thinking we are doing in the quiet of our present days!

It is amazing, when one does begin to consider it, how many kinds of relationships there are, of every depth and degree, in the social settings which frame our lives. But the real relationship, towering above the give-and-take contacts of ordinary living, is that God-given bond of friendship. This is really what you were writing about, but I wish you had said more.

Some wonderful things have been written about friendship through the ages and in every language, and yet how many thousands never experience it because they remain becalmed in their own shallow waters unable, or refusing to give so that they may receive. Many poor souls befriend a succession of dear devoted and totally uncritical dogs or cats rather than perish from emotional starvation. Others, in the icy igloos of their hearts, remain aloof from all creatures. These people are not at once distinguishable because they usually maintain superficial and frivolous contacts that sail under the flag of friendship. But superficiality is the death of love, and without love there is no bond. No intellectual raptures or exchanges can break through our self-centeredness as natural affection and warmth of heart can do.

Friendships usually start as instantaneously as a spark when two flints accidentally strike. Suddenly one is aware of a matching something in another person's mind or make-up, and one is, so to speak, hooked from that second. A friendship may also grow slowly out a shared task or effort of endurance which reveals little by little the qualities of soul—patience, courage, fortitude—that evoke one's esteem and then one's love. Friendship stems, in other words, from an awareness of someone which compels one to "grapple him to one's soul with hoops of steel," as Hamlet said. Thereafter, between true friends there is no "mine and thine," but a constant flow of giving and receiving, making each one richer and more himself than he could ever be alone.

The really heavenly thing about friendship—and it *is* heavenly, heaven sent and heaven blessed—is that it is chosen, consciously and with the entire freedom of our wills. Our families are ready-made; our social setting and

our co-workers are fairly unchangeable. But in a friendship you choose me and I choose you.

Friendship can become an island of comfort and trust for
two at the drop of a hat. It is nothing if not satisfying:
mutual friends share a mutual joy, each draws out a fresh
aspect of the other, thus providing new pleasure for both.

Part of the fun of friendship is being with others, laughing, exchanging ideas and nonsense, turning everything
into a sparkle. Nonetheless, in the final distillation, friendship, like marriage, is for two. Each is drawn to the other so
that their spirits fuse. It is a relationship of confident
abandonment and complete trust. It is never, unless
spoiled by self-love, jealous or possessive or demanding. It
confers complete freedom under whichever face it smiles:
its happy face, its tender face, its giving or receiving face.

I quote this extract from Professor John MacMurray
which I came across in *The Noonday Devil* by Bernard Bas-
sett, SJ:

> If two people are associated merely for what they can get
> out of one another, it obviously is not a friendship. Two
> people are friends because they love one another. That is all
> you can say about it. . . . The impulse to do this is simply the
> impulse to be ourselves completely; not to gain anything, not
> to achieve anything, or to do anything in particular, but
> simply to be ourselves as fully and completely as possible.

Then there are the "friendships" made from reading
books—friendships with people whom one instinctively
likes just from reading anecdotes about them and their
reported sayings. I am thinking of Heloise, St. Teresa of
Avila, and Lady Jane Grey, to name a few among many.
With books I never feel alone. However, reading can be
overdone at first, as I think you too have found; when
recovering from the death of a spouse, one's mind is only
receptive at certain levels.

A friend of mine, a painter, taught me that when suffering from a loss, it is necessary to try to force oneself to be creative—it is a counterbalance and a wonderful help. She had suggested to the authorities at the Royal Marsden Cancer Hospital that she should give painting lessons to those patients who had nothing to do but think about the probable hopelessness of their situations. At first most of them declined, saying that they could not draw at all, and only one or two responded positively. But soon many more joined in, and before long they were eagerly looking forward to these opportunities for self-expression, and my friend told me that some of their productions were quite interesting.

That was a wonderful idea of hers—and she did it while she had four growing children and a husband to think about! You, Diana, are so good at needlework that you could do something like that and open up new horizons for yourself. It is just that initial effort that is so difficult. One needs to be someone like my painter friend who can break the ice and release new painters, potters, writers into the world. These people would then have something real to give, and it might help them to forget their experience of pain.

Enough for now, but write again soon!

M.

\*　　　　\*　　　　\*

Dearest Diana,

It is Saint Valentine's Day today and I have been listening to a radio program's discussion on love—a very difficult thing to discuss because it is as variable as the individuals who experience it. There are so many loves too: of life, of nature, of everything God has created. And within this great glow is the red hot core of love for those special souls who mean everything to us.

The other day I was looking through a book of quotations, and came upon these two from Goethe: "What happiness to be beloved; and O, what bliss to love." And then, "It is a man's failings that make him truly lovable." (I should say it depends on the failings!) A long essay could be written on each of those extracts.

The sad thing is that so many people are afraid to allow their fondness to flower. Fear, used in its sense of "apprehension," is a crippling thing. Applied in its meaning of "reverence" it is of course an essential ingredient of love. Too many people dare not risk the involvement, the gift of themselves (it *is* a risk—pain and rejection may follow—but the risk is nothing compared with the reward); or they may have been wounded too often by the death or loss of those whom they deeply loved to feel they can face it again. This is a natural, self-protective fear, but an ungenerous one when someone who needs them begs to be let in. It seems to me that a cold face and closed heart are the ultimate in selfishness.

In the final analysis, love is trust. It is not passion. Passion is violent and unpredictable, but trust is like a down pillow set on a granite rock.

When you next write, give me your thoughts on the state of old age. Notice that I don't say the "problem," because every state of age has its own problems. Let's have a discussion on old age!

As always,

M.

*        *        *

Dearest Diana,

I was so glad to get your letter about age. If we were wiser we would start thinking it all out much earlier, and so be in some way prepared for it. Probably those old people whom we admire for their *joie de vivre*, or their serenity—or whatever it is in them that attracts us—have done exactly that.

What you say is all very true, but you let yourself be too depressed by it. So do I, although I realize that it should not depress us. Getting on, as they say, is just another experience in life. Even death is such an experience. You can't die unless you have lived (even lived it up!). Neither can you be old without having been young, and what fun that was—sometimes! The whole thing constitutes a different problem for each person. Ideally it should be the time of "mists and mellow fruitfulness"; of gathering in the sheaves from our personal harvests, be they heavy or light, and in the process finding ourselves reaping as we have sown.

But you have not mentioned the two really critical things that make or mar our latter years—to my mind the only things that can justify depressions. Those are poor health and poor circumstances. The busy family woman, or the busy business woman, unless they have made far-sighted preparations and taken up other interests, may already be feeling useless and disoriented. If, on top of this, lumbago makes it difficult for them to move, or arthritis cripples their hands, or cataracts cloud their eyes, they will find it very hard to accept, let alone enjoy their autumn years. They may have friends: career women especially often have many friends. The devoted family woman perhaps fewer, as she may have had no time or interest for special relationships, though some of the daily contacts may have grown deeper roots than she suspected. But without good health, and to a lesser extent money, she will find it very hard to take advantage of one of the real assets of age, which is the freedom it brings with it.

This freedom, after years under the yoke of our calling, is too often unrecognized and unappreciated. It is, of course, also the freedom to be lonely, and very lonely at that. But it allows us to look around, try things out, see what life is made of. Here though, is where circumstance can quench the smoking flax. To be getting older, birthday after birthday, and still to feel fit and vigorous is one thing. But to live like Mr. Micawber, on the wrong side of the necessary sixpence, requires hope and heroic courage if the corrosion of lethargy and despair are to be avoided.

At the same time, even that tragic state of affairs is better than the fate of those aging people who, having the means to employ others to look after their needs, never lift a finger for themselves, and gradually lapse into a state where life is lived from meal to meal, and the only exercise they take is looking at the clock. Even the very old, when they are sensible and independent, can always be making little tasks for themselves to keep their interests alive, moving around with a duster, or shelling peas, or sewing on somebody's buttons.

There is another tiresome thing about the evening years. If one gets ill or has to have an operation, one never seems to recover to the level one was at before. The walks one used to take have become too long, the shopping basket too heavy and so on. Every setback results in another step downward. Of course you did mention this, Diana. I have not yet begun to creak, so have still to experience it, but come it will, all in good time. And the only medicine for these woes is patient acceptance, and the contented remembering of those days when people used to say, "You've got young eyes, please thread this needle," or, "You've got young legs, do run and get my book."

Old age will be much less a time of disappointment and regret if we can manage to be outgoing, interested, and above all unselfish. It is frightening how quickly selfishness establishes itself when we live alone. And I think you are right when you say that the worst enemy is self-pity. The best cure for that is congenial company, which is just what one lacks when one lives alone. Back to Sassoon's sonnet:

Alone...the word is life endured and known.
It is the stillness where our spirits walk
And all but inmost faith overthrown.

Well, there we are. We haven't solved the insoluable, but it is good to shake hands with the facts. We still have time to make our preparations, so let us not fall into a torpor before we have done so!

Always and ever,

M.